In Praise of Shadows Architecture
A Line of Thought

PARK BOOKS

Contents

A Line of Thought 5
In Praise of Shadows

Encompass Darkness 9
Elisabet Yanagisawa

Material and Making 17

Passage of Wood 19
Kayak House 22
Atelier Grytnäs 28
Lindholmen Lab 34
Elma 40
Aesop Bibliotekstan 42
Aesop SoFo 46
Sauna Grytnäs 50
Artbarn 54
Tree House 56

Framing Space 59	Structure as Form 101	Interacting Spaces 143	Index 188
Solbrinken 61	Ca d'Ombra 103	Stockholm City Library 145	
Risön Cabin 70	Loggia d'Ombra 106	DIS Stockholm 150	
In Praise of Loos Loft 74	Loggia Furniture 114	WY13 152	
Guldboda 78	Ör Pavilion 118	Gotlandshem 156	
Storön 82	Rosendal Pavilion 120	The Cords & Co 162	
KIKA Landsort 88	Klockelund 124	Let Me Be Myself 168	
Magelungens Strand 92	Pavilions on Tour 128	Stockholm Winebar 170	
Vega 96	Le Pavillon Hexagonal 130	Bio Rio 174	
	Hexagon H22 134	Visitor Center 178	
	Bridge Kattvikskajen 138	Ulriksdal Cemetery 180	
	Double House 140	Tower of Democracy 186	

A Line of Thought In Praise of Shadows

A thought or an idea never develops into a project in a straight line. Architectural knowledge for us is not only created in the studio, it has to be gained in dialogue with actual materials and building techniques on site, and it is important to us to keep the line of thought from idea to realization so that it is readable when the project is built. In all processes where we are close to the actual production, or actually building ourselves, we believe in the value of following a path meandering its way forward within the project. Knowledge and experiences evolve over time and in trajectories that go beyond the individual projects. We strive to achieve a kinship between our projects for different clients, with different programs and on different sites—the projects feed into each other.

We formed our practice based on common ground gained from study, teaching and travel experiences. Katarina Lundeberg studied at the Architecture School at the Royal Danish Academy in Copenhagen. There she became interested in a process that uses drawing as a tool to develop a project in a coherent form; in architecture as a discipline of creating a consistent form with intentions and proportions readable in plan and section. Fredric Benesch studied at Chalmers University of Technology in Gothenburg, where the ideal of a contextual modernism merged with studies in traditional building techniques to form a vision of architecture with a social agenda, and at the Royal Academy of Art in Stockholm, which represented a vision of an architecture with strong spatial qualities and an identity gained from building technology and materiality.

An important basis of our practice is our experience as a teaching team at the KTH School of Architecture in Stockholm. The teaching challenged us, with our different backgrounds of study and practice, to form a common field and path for our studio. We learned that we share an interest in the intricate architectural play of geometry and perspective found in the Renaissance and the Baroque, having each traveled to Italy to study its art and architecture during our educations. We have continued to build on this interest in our work, not least in four Venice Biennale projects that

Loggia d'Ombra with
Loggia Bench and Table.
On display at the
Venice Biennale.

all have a relation to classical architecture. The architectural culture of Graubünden in Switzerland is another common interest that we have discovered and found valuable. It is an architecture very much based on site, materiality and construction, and we have continued to explore it through field trips and dialogue with local architects and engineers.

To us, the most important part of an architectural education is to understand the importance of the line of thought, how the hard work with drawings actually creates real spaces and how these spaces are defined by matter and structure, finding their punctuation in details. An idea should be reflected in the project as a whole but also in the details. Over the years, our firm has had many competent employees and collaborators who have made invaluable contributions, and our role as founding partners is to be the guiding architects, ensuring that we stay on the path and continue our line of thought. In the process we have learned the value of daring to be personal rather than general. The core ambition of our practice is to achieve a sustainable architecture consistent in geometry and material and with a character of its own. We learn and develop in smaller projects where we can be more experimental, such as those for the Biennale in Venice and for private clients. As the projects grow in scale, our mission is to keep creating architecture that is characterized by a consistent line of thought and that adds qualities to its site, its users and its surroundings. Our best tool to do this is to stay very present in the projects and work in close collaboration with clients, carpenters and builders.

We are grateful to have borrowed our studio name from Junichirō Tanizaki's book *In Praise of Shadows* (*In'ei raisan*, 1933). We appreciate his fine descriptions of architectonic values that, to us, are fundamental, as well as his humoristic play with the meaning and responsibility of tradition and architecture. We discovered the book when we were teaching together, and thus the name of our office has also become an important constant reminder of where we come from and that architecture is about putting a sustainable shadow

The mark of architecture is to put a sustainable shadow on the surface of the earth.

on the surface of the earth. We are happy to be able to include an essay by Elisabet Yanagisawa, PhD student at HDK in Gothenburg and guest lecturer at Konstfack and Beckmans in Stockholm. We share an interest in Japanese architecture and film, as well as in the abovementioned book by Tanizaki. Through her knowledge and research, we gain a new, deeper perspective on Japanese aesthetics and architecture.

We have grouped our work into four chapters: *Material and Making* deals with the inherent qualities and characteristics of materials, how they can be worked and how they behave over time; *Framing Space* deals with the spatial relation between inside and outside, setting the stage for the drama; *Structure as Form* reflects our philosophy that architecture and structure are one, everything is structure, everything is architecture and everything is visible; and *Interacting Spaces* focuses on the interaction of the users with the space and with each other, where a common strategy has been to work with material qualities for a elevated experience of presence.

Katarina Lundeberg & Fredric Benesch
Founding Architects
In Praise of Shadows Architecture

Encompass Darkness Elisabet Yanagisawa

In modernity there exists a preconception that light is equivalent to enlightenment and rational thinking. That all that is dark and dusky must go, be lit up with a blowtorch. A conception of total transparency as the highest ideal of systems, methods and theories. The contemporary ideal has become to design buildings that let in a maximum amount of light. Outer walls are glass fronts through which you are exposed from outside, as if you are living within a shop window. Few question the notion of ubquituous light, since we live in a time characterized by rational thought and transparency.

The Japanese writer Junichirō Tanizaki did not share this opinion. In the text *In Praise of Shadows*, published in 1933, he advocated the idea that darkness is as necessary as light. The actual subject matter, the praise of shadows, is a hymn to everything vague and dark, to the hidden and only half-visible. Tanizaki writes about it in a way that on first reading can seem like a string of associations. This is precisely his intention: he draws us inside an atmospheric world, filled with example upon example of places that lie in shadow and darkness. He takes us to the inner rooms of a Japanese house. Within it we experience rooms that, if you raise your eyes between the beams in the ceiling, breathe compact darkness. The low shelf of the *tokonoma* almost floats above the dim tatami floor. Shadowy corners and solitary kerosene lamps glow in pitch-black darkness. Outside toilets facing north are enshrouded in shady thickets. Furnishings are in dark wood, while the play of shadows in different hues can be made out against sand-colored walls. He describes the sensation of gazing down into a shiny, black lacquer bowl, in which one can make out the golden flecks on the bottom through the half-transparent miso soup.

> The quality that we call beauty, however, must always grow from the realities of life, and our ancestors, forced to live in dark rooms, presently came to discover beauty in shadows, ultimately to guide shadows towards beauty's ends.[1]

Tanizaki imparts a very serious teaching. He instructs us in something that already in the 1930s was about to get lost in Japan: the classical Japanese view of beauty, where the play of monochrome shadows and the obscurity of darkness constitute the highest level of aesthetic experience.

According to filmmaker J.F. Martel and music professor Phil Ford,[2] *In Praise of Shadows* is a meditation on the metaphysical, political and artistic cost of the modern fear of the dark. They suggest that Tanizaki's essay is highly topical in our time as it opens a door into a world we have forgotten in which darkness is present. This insight reveals that something highly alive is missing in our contemporary environment and lifestyle. In all our eagerness to embrace the rational, we have taken away something existential. We have taken away the shadows and the darkness in our existence. The houses we live in have no dark corners for integrity and reflection. The kinds of shadows and darkness Tanizaki describes are not there to be experienced in contemporary architecture. The houses are lit throughout. The city streets are bathed in light; at night you can't see the constellations.

Tanizaki wants the reader to awaken and realize what an aesthetic feeling is. In everyday life we don't talk about what aesthetic feelings mean. If aesthetics are addressed at all it is most often in visual terms. *Aisthesis* means to perceive through the senses, that is, through our bodily sensations: it is not an intellectual analytical ability. Classical Japanese aesthetics are about letting the senses work symphonically, multisensorially, not each on their own. In that way an aesthetic feeling arises as an actual bodily experience outside language. The aesthetic feeling can be expressed in sound, for example in the form of surprising, spontaneous exclamations like Brrrr! Oh, wow! Eee! Mmm! Nnnn! What is expressed can be a pleasant feeling, enjoyment, a rigid feeling of coldness, a melting, relaxed feeling of warmth, a pricking sting from an insect, a sharp edge, a surprising, harmonious sensation, or an aching, heavy pain. The feeling can be a strong sensation of joy or a calm and harmonious sensation of care and warmth, or, just as likely, a scary sense of dread or an insistent feeling of unease. It can be a captivating feeling of beauty or a persuasive feeling of belonging. We experience things like these daily, but how do we let them impact our knowledge of the world?

Aesthetic feeling involves sensations we have from several senses simultaneously. Like when gazing up at the starlit sky on a dark, cold but clear night at full moon; or when in a pitch-black house with just a single candle, something that happens perhaps only when the power is out after a storm in the countryside. Or the feeling of sitting by a campfire with tall dark tree trunks behind you and unknown sounds in the night. Each aesthetic feeling is a singular affect, a unique quality. Aesthetic quality is a concept in itself. It cannot be replaced, just like one code cannot be replaced with another, or one concept with some other arbitrary concept. Each singular feeling of this kind is an affective quality, a haecceity, as Gilles Deleuze would have said. A haecceity is an impersonal affect that takes place: like a rhythm, a natural occurrence, snowflakes falling in darkness, rain drizzling in shadows or lashing against dark window panes, or wind howling in the dark night. Hence each haecceity is not a subjective feeling but a singular moment. We can notice haecceities, discern them with our senses. They can only be lived, experienced, not be thought or cognitively analyzed.

The darkness is one such sensorial haecceity, an aesthetic feeling. It is an actual experience of singular presence. The darkness is not just a place devoid of light. The darkness accommodates a host of sensations of different kinds which are non-visual. I can move in a dark house and more acutely feel the massive wooden floorboards under my feet. I feel the sneaking paws of the cat on the staircase, hear her scratching on the porch. In the darkness I hear the crackling in the fireplace as if through an amplifier, I feel the quiet in the room settling like a fragrance. The shadows drift in on a cellular level, into my molecules.

[1] Junichiro Tanizaki, *In Praise of Shadows*, London: Vintage Books, 1977 [*In'ei raisan*, 1933], p. 29.

[2] *Weird Studies*, podcast, episode 101, "Our Fear of the Dark: On Tanizaki's *In Praise of Shadows*," June 23, 2021.

[3] *Jinkō* is the highest quality of agarwood, an extremely fragrant resin which is used as incense. In the Middle East it is called *oud*.

Silver Pavilion (Ginkaku-ji), Kyoto, Japan

Tea masters like Sen no Rikyū (1522–1591) knew very well that darkness enhances the sharpness of other senses. That was why the tea room should be kept dusky, in order not to let the eye and sight dominate. The tea ceremony was framed so that other sensations could enter, such as the subtle touch of the lips against the tea bowl's edge, the fragrance of *jinkō*[3] incense, the sound of simmering water on the embers, and the bitter taste of *matcha* tea, which keeps the mind clear. The room of shadows enhances an atmosphere that is non-linguistic, sensory and even metaphysical. The tea ceremony was actually a lesson in aesthetic feeling, in the art of cultivating multi-sensibility as aesthetic self-cultivation. Aesthetic self-cultivation is an act that is repeated over and over again, a training in sharpening the senses; a practical meditation in order for the body, mind and soul to find harmony, precisely in order to be able to develop one's ability to know oneself. The idea of the tea ceremony is that the commonplace is sufficiently advanced; to practice perfection in the repetitive act. This is a Buddhist thought that takes its departure from the middle, *in medias res*, the middle of life where you stand, in the commonplace. Sweep the floor, rake the leaves, peel the potatoes, boil the rice, prepare the tea, sharpen the pencil, grate the Japanese ink, over and over again; practice in order to do this in the most perfect way. The tea master's practice demonstrates this in the best way by showing with the body, through the act itself, rather than by telling or lecturing. The darkness constitued the backdrop against which these acts and practices played out. Together, as a collective experience, one shared these aesthetic feelings. One sharpened the senses in common, and words expressing assent and affirmation were more like communicative signals, signs in a complex web of concordance.

What Tanizaki wants us to wake up to is that our ancestors had a natural feeling for this densified, mild darkness where you come into deep resonance with the innermost spirit of existence. This of course does not apply only to Japan. That feeling cannot be reduced to language, because it is an affect, a bodily feeling that is rather an attunement, a vibration. You cannot see the light in the foreground if there is no background of darkness against which the light appears. Light and darkness are always in interplay, in a play of powers. They are like yin and yang, constantly turning into one another and retransformed through continuous processes, to different beats, in different patterns and repetitions.

An excess of light leaves no space for contemplation and integrity. A constant abundance of light that never goes out is comparable to the most trivial circumstance of life you can imagine: a convenience store with fluorescent lights open around the clock, a symbol of the illumined surface of meaninglessness, rooms with blinding surfaces without shadows. Places that repel the delicate, the fair, the subtle. The mind is also a place that needs to be cultivated actively, given conditions for development. The mind must be able to rest in peaceful darkness and half-shadows in order to be able to think clear thoughts.

The appreciation of the world of shadows has different names in different cultures. In France you enter *l'heure bleue* toward the end of the day. A time of transformation, the whole landscape changes its form and is colored with blue veils. In Italy artists like Leonardo da Vinci and Caravaggio appreciated the strong contrasts between light and dark, *chiaroscuro*. In Sweden we have an old expression, *kura skymning*, "to huddle at dusk," which means to let the eyes rest in the transitional shadows when day turns into evening. You must not be too quick to light all the electric lamps.

In Greek mythology it is Nyx, Night, who according to Hesiod gives birth to Hemera, Day. Darkness comes before light. Light is born out of darkness. If you consider the analogy with background and foreground, both are needed in a dualistic world. They are complements and preconditions for one another; the tension between dual qualities upholds the world. Darkness is needed just as much as light.

You might think that Tanizaki's world is fragmented. Example follows example, symbol is added to symbol. But all these detailed demonstrations are necessary in order for us to be able to grasp what he means. Affects are actual singular elements, that is, it is the detail that is the message, irreducibly. Altogether the details form the atmosphere. The fragmentariness is reminiscent of another classical thinker in Western culture, Heraclitus. His collected *Fragments* consist of a series of short statements. They might seem to be disparate propositions, but if closely meditated upon, and having zoomed out, they actually constitute parts of a greater puzzle. Aesthetic feeling appears as spontaneous cracks in the habitual, as fragments. Each fragment expresses more than the whole. Is this really possible? Yes, if the fragments are experienced, in contrast to a purely propositional whole that one has not experienced oneself.

Tanizaki's aesthetic style comes from ancient Chinese and Japanese philosophy, influenced by the concept of beauty, *yūgen*. The sign for *yūgen* comes from the Daoist philosophy of yin and yang. *Yū* stands for yin, a mysterious, enigmatic, dark beauty.[4] The literary scholar Michael Marra explains that "*Yūgen* is something well beyond the reach of man's immediate perception and understanding, since it is too deep and too far for humans to reach, even conceptually."[5] *Yūgen* came to indicate the other world, or the Daoist Way and also the Buddhist enlightenment. It also hints at a world beyond dualism, a cosmic level of beauty that transcends the customary and the known.

Yūgen flourished in the court life of the Heian culture of Japan. The fictional epic *The Tale of Genji* was written during this period, more than thousand years ago, by the court lady Murasaki Shikibu. The emperor's court lived in a world of grace and refinement in old Kyoto. The court palace was built as a series of empty rooms that could change character by means of verandas, sliding doors, folding walls and screens. In these rooms of shadow one practiced different arts that were half hidden, half suggested: letter writing, poetry and moon gazing.

4 "The compound *yūgen* (lit. depth and mystery) is made of two Chinese characters: *yū* means 'faint, dim' and also 'deep'; *gen* indicates the black color, the color of heaven, something far away, something quiet and an occult principle. We find the character *gen* used in the *Dao de jing* (Classic of the Way and Integrity) to describe the 'Way': 'These two—the nameless and what is named—emerge from the same source yet are referred to differently. Together they are called obscure (Ch. *xuan*; Jpn. *gen*).'"
Michael F. Marra, *Japan's Frames of Meaning: A Hermeneutic Reader*, Honolulu: University of Hawai'i Press, 2011, p. 173.

5 Ibid.

6 Tanizaki, *In Praise of Shadows*, p. 32

7 Steve Odin, *Artistic Detachment in Japan and the West*, Honolulu: University of Hawai'i Press, 2001, p. 17

More than three hundred years later, the playwright Zeami Motokiyo (1363–1443) continued to be inspired by *yūgen* in creating a multi-sensory drama called *Noh*. He considered *yūgen* to be the highest ideal of perfection in many arts. In the concept of *yūgen* there is no fearful, negative darkness. The darkness in *yūgen* is an inner depth, an intuitive, quiet feeling for nature, a sense of the cosmic. The Western concept of the sublime perhaps comes closest to *yūgen*. What is interesting in Zeami's development of *yūgen* is that he creates a scale of nine degrees of *yūgen*. He describes in detail a progression of different kinds of beauty. At the lower levels it is colorful and playful, at the higher levels it shades into monochrome, detached, and at the highest level it is surreal.

If we recall that night is the backdrop, and cosmos is space, then the backdrop is dark and enigmatic, as much for us today as it was for the Heian court a thousand years ago.

A Japanese room might be likened to an ink wash painting, the paper-paneled shoji being the expanse where the ink is thinnest, and the alcove where it is darkest. [...] I marvel at our comprehension of the secrets of shadows, our sensitive use of shadow and light. For the beauty of the alcove [*tokonoma*] is not the work of some clever device. An empty space is marked off with plain wood and plain walls, so that the light drawn into it forms dim shadows within emptiness. There is nothing more. And yet, when we gaze into the darkness that gathers behind the crossbeam, around the flower vase, beneath the shelves, though we know perfectly well it is mere shadow, we are overcome with the feeling that in this small corner of the atmosphere there reigns complete and utter silence; that here in the darkness immutable tranquility holds sway.⁶

The Japanese traditional space is constructed to be a metaphysical experience of sensibility. The space in itself becomes the place of existence, the place to experience the highest realms of aesthetics, an embodied void. Darkness as a cosmic void reappears over and over again in Buddhist and Daoist metaphysics.

In our everyday concrete world, we need to relate to opposites: warm—cold, up—down, right—left and so on. This reality and this way of thinking is dualism. When in Japanese and Chinese metaphysics one talks about nondualism one is concerned with transcending this dichotomy. The concepts of emptiness and nothingness both relate to a way of thinking that seeks to transcend the relative, the dualistic. This is *dao*, also called nonbeing, the nameless and formless, in Japanese *mu* (Chinese *wu*). In the Japanese tradition of Zen Buddhism, the concept of *mushin* (no-mind) is applied to the aesthetic experience of beauty in art and nature.⁷ I would like to say that the concept of nothingness, *mu*, and other related concepts like *mushin* are liberated from both the relative and the absolute, by encompassing them both, in a noncontradictory state. The symbo of *mu* is the circle, *ensō*.

Nanzen-ji,
Kyoto, Japan

The concept of *ku* is a Buddhist concept meaning emptiness. *Ku* is most often translated as void but also means sky or heaven. Bodily, *ku* represents spirit, thought and also creative energy. The concept of *ku* also deals with language and the gap between concepts and their supposed referents, maintaining that we cannot reach reality through conceptual means alone.[8]

According to this way of thinking there are states of being that cannot be expressed in words. In order to grasp these experiences, because it is a practice, one needs to find other ways of experiencing them, such as bodily, through the senses. It is also possible to use language to express states or observations that are, for example, paradoxical and nondualistic. Haiku is one means of expressing this kind of experience. Another is to regard existence as a stylized painting in *sumi*, Japanese ink, where the concrete and the abstract together reach a different or superimposed level of meaning. In Japanese culture there are several different ways to try to reach such states by means of artistic practices, as a kind of self-cultivation, meditation in movement.

According to a Buddhist view of beauty, the highest beauty is to transcend dualism. It is neither beautiful nor ugly: that kind of thinking is dualistic. This is also related to light and darkness. A famous Zen dialogue between a monk and his teacher says:

Chao-chou: In which are you, in the light or the dark?
Monk: I am in neither.
Chao-chou: Are you between the two then?
Monk: I am not there either.
Chao-chou: Then you simply dwell in the words "neither in the light nor in the dark nor in between"?
Monk: I am master of those words and employ them.
Chao-chou: That is the answer I wanted to hear.[9]

Tanizaki is brimming with the thought of moving in this nondualistic sphere as a human being and artist. His aesthetic ideal is not subjective but a perspective that is beyond the subject, nonhuman; in Japanese it is called *hininjō*, detachment from human emotions. With this as an ideal, however, you need also to relate, in parallel, the human emotional perspective of *sympathy*. The themes of Tanizaki's writings move between these poles, detachment from humanity (*hininjō*) and sympathy (*aware*).

Today, in philosophy and different artistic practices, new ways of moving in a sphere akin to Tanizaki's and of exploring a nondualistic perspective have arisen. It is about questioning a dualistic way of thinking that fetters our thoughts, inherited historically from a polarized Aristotelian mode of thinking in terms of either/or. Thinking outside the given, the habitual, the known, is about not just moving within some representation, about thinking outside the so-called box. What shape can these modes take?

The Dutch philosopher of new materialism Rick Dolphijn discusses contemporary thinkers who move in a Tanizakian world.

8 T.P. Kasulis, *Zen Action/Zen Person*, Honolulu: University of Hawai'i Press, 1981, p. 23

9 Sōetsu Yanagi, *The Unknown Craftsman: A Japanese Insight into Beauty*, Tokyo, New York, London: Kodansha, 1972, p. 138.

10 Rick Dolphijn, *The Philosophy of Matter: A Meditation*, London: Bloomsbury Academic, 2021, pp. 73–103.

11 *Gestalten* [verb, German] and *gestalta* [verb, Swedish] are precisely such incommensurable words. In artistic contexts they should be kept in their German or Swedish form, since there is no equivalent word in English.

12 Junichiro Tanizaki, *Till skuggornas lov,* translation and postscript by Vibeke Emond, Lund: Ellerströms förlag, 1998 [*In'ei raisan*, 1933], p. 66.

Here it is not just a matter of thinking "otherness." Otherness still resides in dualistic thinking. Dolphijn seizes upon the contemporary writer Haruki Murakami's world, where two characters are often set against each other. One represents the rational subject who thinks differently, but still within the box, dualistically. The other character is not irrational but rather nondualistic. They move in a landscape that resembles Tanizaki's shadowy world, where unexpected things happen as a string of synchronicities. Each event leads to the next, like fragments of a larger puzzle, a magical reality.[10]

Yūgen is an aesthetic concept that encompasses darkness as enlightenment through beauty. There are no similar aesthetic concepts in Western philosophy. Consequently, the concept of *yūgen* cannot be translated. Some words and concepts are untranslatable between different languages. In Japanese aesthetics there are quite a few concepts that are incommensurable in this way. Consequently, these must not be reduced to rough mistranslations or careless substitutes, which only partly convey their meaning. Aesthetic concepts especially need to be kept as they are within their cultural fields, and we need to increase our knowledge of aesthetic concepts from different cultures. With such tools we receive widened possibilities for *Gestaltung*[11] within architecture and design.

Tanizaki's view was that as a writer one should utilize the essence of language to the maximum. The essence of the Japanese language is precisely to be able to express vagueness, in a way that is refined, even brilliant. This linguistic mode of communicating vaguely is not something unclear; on the contrary, it is intellectually and aesthetically highly advanced, nuanced, ambiguous precisely in order to express experiences that cannot easily be captured within language. It is an artistic, poetic way of expressing aesthetic and sensible experiences. Tanizaki does this quite brilliantly in a structured format, almost like a "mathematical construction," according to his Swedish translator Vibeke Emond.[12]

Tanizaki is a useful and relevant entryway if you want to explore and develop aesthetic feeling together with an artistic practice. If you have started to open the door to nondualism there are some new (old) methods to develop one's aesthetic practice. Perhaps one of the most fascinating can be to go back in history. As Giorgio Agamben says, the contemporary thinker must be both in the archaic and in the contemporary to be able to think freely.

Contemporariness is, then, a singular relationship with one's own time, which adheres to it and, at the same time, keeps a distance from it. More precisely, it is that relationship with time that adheres to it through a disjunction and an anachronism. Those who coincide too well with their epoch, those who are perfectly tied to it in every respect, are not contemporaries, precisely because they are not capable of seeing it; they are not able to firmly hold their gaze on it.

Material and Making

Passage of Wood

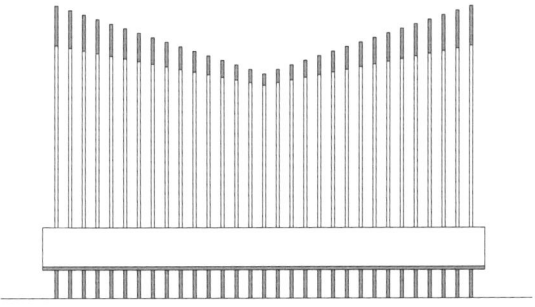 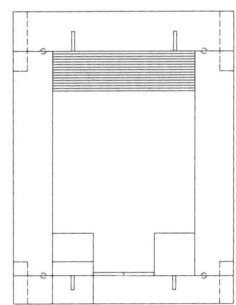

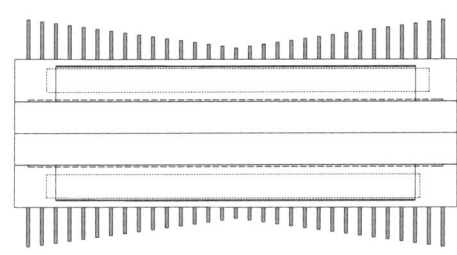

Passage of Wood originated in an assignment from *Wallpaper*. For the task we were teamed up with Danish wooden floor producer Dinesen and the Austrian handicraft organization Werkraum Bregenzerwald. Our task was to create a structure that could be a meeting place within the exhibition space. Originally displayed at the Wallpaper Handmade exhibition at Salone del Mobile Milano 2014, the passage was later shown at the Venice Biennale, as well as at Werkraum Bregenzerwald. Passage of Wood is a spatial structure illustrating the fundamental architectonic principles investigated by the project. The passage is constructed from large wooden beams and planks, with all parts cut from a solid piece of wood. The frames are glued, all other joints are made of wood, and the passage is assembled like a wooden puzzle with the weight of the large beams ensuring the stability of the structure. The passage is designed to enhance the contrast between the planks that frame the space and the massive beams from which they originate. When viewed diagonally, the massive Douglas planks have a solid appearance; as you walk through the structure, it transforms into something more transparent. The gradually changing width of the frames increases the transparency of the structure and the visibility of the massive beams toward the center of the passage, where the height is also at its lowest. (2014)

Douglas fir Douglas fir is a fir species that grows in Central Europe and America. The wood for the passage is sourced from the Black Forest region in Germany, where they cut down one tree at a time, conducting sustainable forest management. The wood has a reddish color and anise scent, which gives a strong character to the structure. There are few knots, and the layers of each year's growth are clear, creating a calm atmosphere. In the original design for Milan, Passage of Wood featured two Douglas fir tree trunks as benches— a tribute to the origins of the wood. However, the trunks were too heavy for Palazzo Bembo, the fifteenth-century palace where it was installed in Venice, so they were exchanged for a wider floor and passage.

(previous spread)
Drawings 1:100.

(above)
On display at the
Venice Biennale.

Structure In the hull of a boat, the many curved components are attached to a spine, extending upward and outward to form the framework of the hull. It is a structural principle that combines functional and aesthetic values, creating curved shapes as the geometry of the parts transforms along the structure. Architectural arrangements such as these, where form is developed through structural principles, are important points of reference for us. Using a constructive order provides a spatial quality and clear understanding of architecture, and it also teaches us to use material in an economical way.

(left)
During assembly at the workshop in the Bregenzerwald.

(right)
Display in Milan with the massive benches installed.

Kayak House

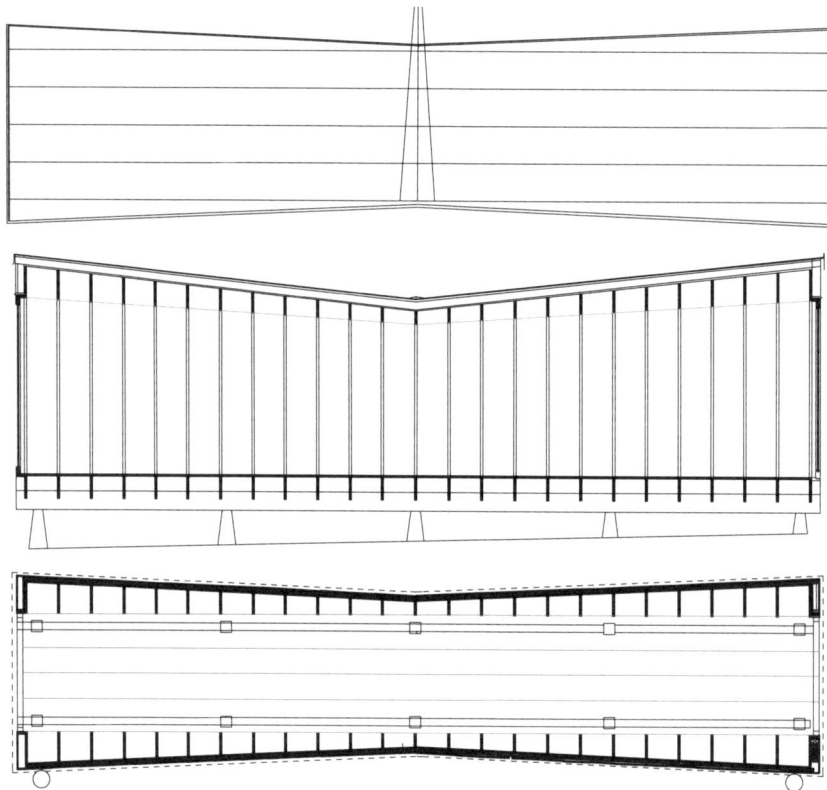

The Kayak House is built from the reused structure of Passage of Wood. After being exhibited in Milan, Venice and the Bregenzerwald, it was mounted a fourth time at its final destination in the Swedish archipelago. The construction is the framework of the Passage stretched three times. The interior is clad with fine birch plywood and an oak floor. The facade is made from eight local pine trees cut down at the site. The three trunks were cut with a chainsaw on a saw line, and because of their conical shape the planks were assembled like a puzzle in order to use as much of the wood as possible. The house stands among blueberry bushes on a slope by the water and is placed as sensitively as possible with a minimum of groundworks. Similar to the way barns or sea sheds were traditionally placed on granite plinths, it rests on ten plinths made of concrete cast on site. The structure is clad with birch plywood and linen insulation, and the facade is treated with a silica-based treatment. The oak door windows were made by a local carpenter.

The original inspiration to reuse the structure of the former pavilion came from the beautiful construction drawings of the Swedish kayak and boat designer Björn Thomassen. They inspired the transformation of the structure, which was already more like the hull of a boat than a structure for a house, and gave it its new shape and purpose. (2018)

Tactility In the early days of the wood industry, frame saws left marks on the wooden planks they produced, but today it is rare to find sawmills that still use a frame saw. In our process we cut down eight pine trees on site, in the month of February when the humidity is low and the moon is full. To avoid damage to the site, we had a carpenter process the trunks in situ with a chainsaw. This gave the planks their rough surface, creating a beautiful play of light and shadow on the facade. The planks were dried and turned outside for a year on the site. Using the whole width of the tree trunk was both economical and gave us a variation of harder core wood and the softer wood on the periphery, creating a difference in the aging process of the planks. To prevent them from bending, and to harmonize with the idea of the local and traditional in dialogue with the modern, the long planks needed to be screwed to the wooden lath; the facade was also screwed on and plugged.

(previous spread left)
Roofplan, section, floorplan 1:100.

(previous spread right)
Structural frames of Douglas fir; floor and window frames in oak.

(opposite page)
Facade of wooden planks from trees cut on site with a chainsaw for a rough surface.

(left)
The wooden kayaks that dictated the length of the house.

(right)
Study model.

Roof of copper: the fifth facade from above, visible from the hill.

Foundation on conical concrete plinths and a facade of conical wooden boards to maximize the use of the trees felled on site.

Atelier Grytnäs

In Grytnäs, a studio to work and live in was added to an existing summer house setting for several generations of one family. A careful placement on a rock with a view to the north was chosen. It is an experimental house for the architect and her family, with three small bedrooms, a main living space and a bathroom with a view of the sky—a minimal house of 40 square meters in the tradition of "less is more." The concrete walls and chimney stand as the foundation plinth for the studio. The cross-laminated timber (CLT) construction was planned and structured in a sustainable way so that no other construction was needed, and the boards were used with a minimum of cut-outs. The atelier has a facade panel made using a traditional frame saw, a large window to the north and a long-lasting copper roof. The CLT boards were glued at the meeting points of the planks, which creates beautiful cracks in a varied distribution. (2020)

Local modern tradition The southern archipelago of Lisö boasts some interesting houses built by architects for their own use, from the early establishment of summer houses in the late 1930s onwards. The long landmass of Lisö, which had belonged to the estate Fållnäs Gård, was subdivided and sold as vacation home plots along the rocky coast between the 1920s and 1940s. The Eskil Sundahl summer house at Kalvnäs, which he built in around 1940, Gunnar Asplund's house in Stennäs from 1937, and an interesting house by Ralph Erskine with a consistent use of steel plate are examples of noteworthy architects' houses in the area. These projects have been an inspiration in regard to how to relate to the site and the landscape. The houses have a sensitive relation to the rocks, and some of them have a focused main space with a framed view toward the water. The mass of the house is shaped in a concentrated volume, creating a specific form almost like a stranded ship, adding a sense of movement to the slope.

Sfumato Developed during the Renaissance, sfumato is a painting technique used to create a soft picture with blurred shading and color transitions. In architecture, a patina that develops naturally over time has the same quality: copper that turns brownish or green, or a wooden facade that ages naturally with lines of metallic nails made from oiled steel. Similarly, we wanted the interior to melt together in a warm and soft "sfumato" atmosphere, echoing the colors of the wood and the cliff outside. Repurposed ash floorboards, with their visible joints providing "shadows," were used for the kitchen cabinets and a staircase to the loft. The former floor planks also became a table with the same white oil treatment. The interior is a test lab for different paints and surface treatments. White linseed oil and an emulsion paint with heavy gray pigment, Stucco Lustro, in the bathroom gives a smooth surface that reflects the light from the skylight. Made out of marble powder, it is a surface often used in the entrance halls of apartment buildings in Stockholm but is also commonly used on walls in Italy.

(previous spread left)
An interesting typology close by that has provided inspiration for several projects is the vacation home Kalvnäs by Eskil Sundahl, built around 1940.

A reference for a sensitive placement in the landscape is the summer house Stennäs at Lisö by Gunnar Asplund, built in 1937.

(previous spread right)
Exterior materials include concrete, wood and copper.

(opposite page)
An interior in different grays
with a white-oiled ash floor.

A view to the north that gives
a soft northern working light.

Cross-Laminated Timber (CLT) The intriguing possibilities that a massive wooden material like CLT offers an architect have to be balanced with technical and economic aspects. An advantage of CLT is that it can be used as walls, beams and slabs to form a structure where loads are handled in a wise and sustainable way. In smaller projects, CLT slabs are a challenge during planning in relation to transportation and assembly on site. We consulted the producer as well as the structural engineer to optimize the construction, a limitation being that the crane could only handle a certain load with a distance of 20 meters. The precision and sharp details in how the wooden slabs are put together are an architect's dream. The solid feeling that CLT gives a house like this, on a windy site, is another of its unique qualities.

Evening sun on the western facade fitted tight to the rock.

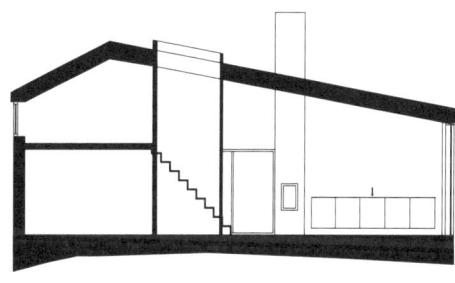

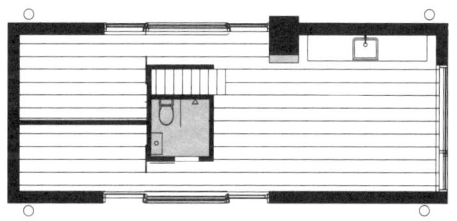

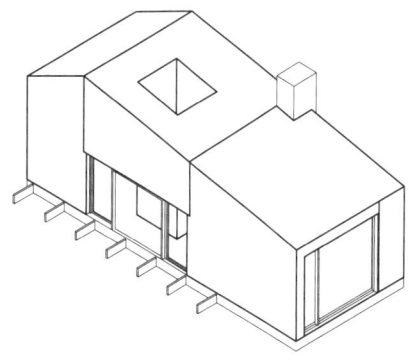

(top to bottom)
Section and plan 1:200.
Axonometric view showing
the CLT boards 1:200.
(left)
CLT under construction.

Lindholmen Lab

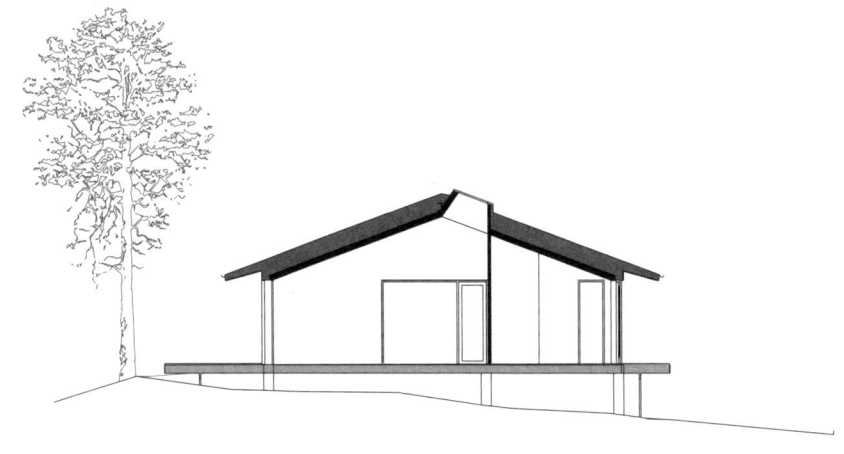

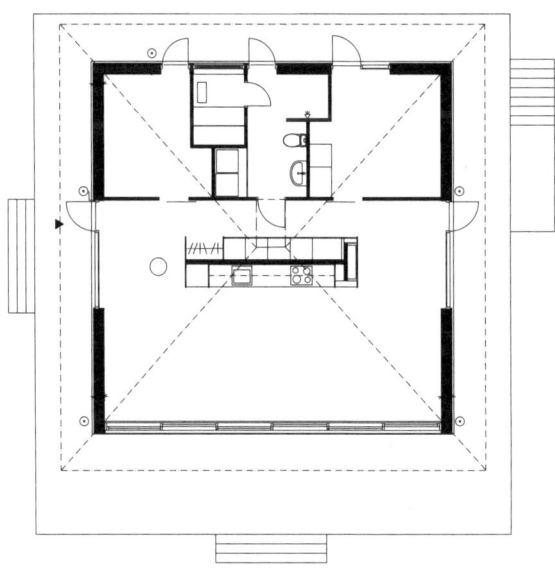

Lindholmen Lab was built as a second home for an energetic couple and their visiting friends: a new house on the site where childhood summers had been spent. He is a researcher in the medical field, she is a health consultant. Getting closer to a period in life with more leisure time, they were planning on spending more time in the archipelago and wanted a place to live and work and enjoy outdoor activities. The plan is almost square to fit the house onto the site and it has a large opening toward the sea. The pyramid roof keeps the roofline low so as not to obscure the neighbors' view and to create a protecting roof on all sides. The proportions of the plan are tailored to integrate a skylight into the geometry of the roof. The house is raised above the highest point of the cliff to preserve the rock and to create a generous view. The wooden deck surrounding the house separates it visually from the ground in a Japanese manner, meeting the rock with austere stairs, also in wood. The house has a silicate treatment on the facade with a gray pigment, a black sheet metal roof and wooden windows. (2020)

Section and plan 1:200.

(opposite page)
View from the water.

The house sits on the ground with a floating terrace and stairs that meet the rock.

The terrace facing
the view to the sea.

Cross-Laminated Timber (CLT) A CLT construction of Martinssons wood elements, constructed with Limträteknik in Falun, was used. The pyramidal clear form is made of a free-bearing CLT structure developed to allow for a rooflight, as well as a generous opening toward the water. Walls are placed as a spatial as well as a structural system of closed and open, and formed to limit cut-outs and waste from the CLT production. The walls and roof are then insulated and clad with wooden panels and a metal roof on site. The interior gets its unified character from the exposed CLT walls and ceiling, and the oiled ash floor. Sliding doors also made from CLT are hung in the walls, and the fittings for these as well as electrical installations are in a contrasting black. The dark gray kitchen, which also integrates the air exchange heater, is formed as a central space divider.

A pyramidal CLT construction with freestanding kitchen.

(opposite page, top to bottom)
Half the house opens up to the terrace facing south.
CLT core under construction.
Diagram 1:400 showing the CLT boards.

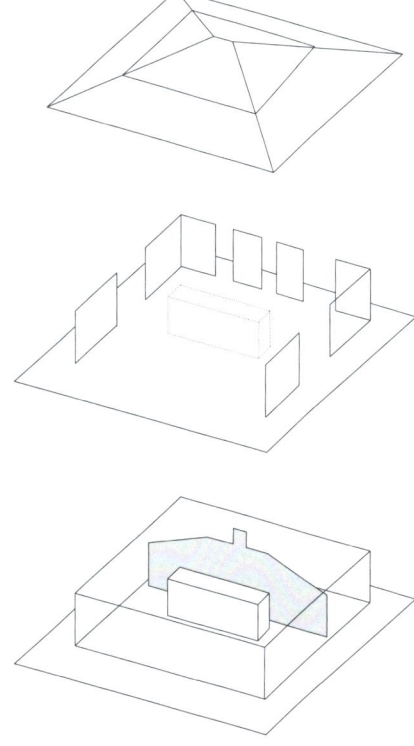

Elma

At the 2012 Venice Biennale, our task for the exhibition *Light Houses* was to create an architectural object commenting on the Nordic Pavilion by Sverre Fehn (1962). On an earlier field trip with students to visit Fehn in his office, he said that traveling is the most important part of becoming and being an architect. Only on a scale of 1:1 are you able to see and understand how buildings are put together. We analyzed the Nordic Pavilion in Venice with these words in mind. The structural concrete beams, both rational and poetic, are dimensioned to create a roof that shades the exhibited objects, blocking out all direct sunlight. The pavilion was once built around a number of trees in the garden, although only a few of them are still in place today. Our project, Elma, played with the idea of putting back one tree, this time sculpted and formed.

As the Nordic Pavilion was once shaped in relation to the trees on site, Elma is a homage in reverse in wood, drawing its geometry from the pavilion. Elma is cut out of an elm tree that grew on Djurgården, the Royal National Park in Stockholm, over the past 103 years. One of the last standing elm trees in Europe of this age, it was infected with Dutch elm disease and had to be cut down the same year. The piece of wood, no longer growing, is turned horizontally, exposing its wooden heart. Elma was formed by chainsaw and hand tools by wood artist Lies-Marie Hoffmann. On some of the cut surfaces the rough marks of the chainsaw remain visible, while others are polished to expose the vivid patterns and colors of the elm wood. Butterfly joints were also formed in relation to the 30/60-degree geometry of the corner pillar of the pavilion, and schematic symbols of the geometry were carved into the surface. (2012)

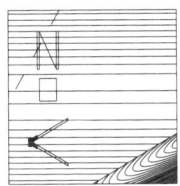

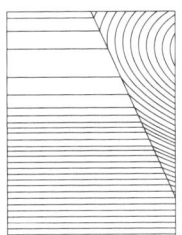  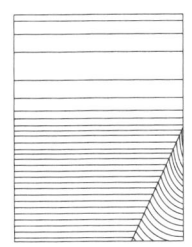

(opposite page)
Carvings in the polished surface were created using a hammer and chisel.

(left)
A volume cut into a shape that is an interpretation of the geometry of the Nordic Pavilion by Sverre Fehn. Our story told by the symbols on the top and sides 1:20.

(right)
Elma was positioned in the pavilion to replace one of the trees that once stood there.

Aesop Bibliotekstan

The starting point for this project was a happy coincidence—Junichirō Tanizaki's philosophy and his book *In Praise of Shadows* was also an important point of reference for the Aesop team. To us it became an opportunity to dig deeper into the book, as well as into spatial thinking in traditional Japanese architecture. It is a tradtion that uses the tatami mat as a system for proportions. A proportion that can be turned 90 degrees or divided into smaller parts, the tatami mat translates the grammar of architecture into a readable system to learn from. It creates a grid that serves as a guideline to the space, defining its borders and how they connect to the outside, as well as the division of the surfaces. Within the grid, scale, mass and materiality became our tools to create a space. We wanted it to be comfortable, inviting and, despite its small size, a rich, tactile experience and sequence of spaces. Wood and plaster shape a space that is divided in two: the active front of the store and the calmer back, where you are invited to sit down—the open and the intimate. The floor, the walls and the ceiling of the inner space are clad in large pieces of solid oak. Using a chainsaw and a chisel, wood artist Lies-Marie Hoffmann cut the three functional pieces out of reused elm timber from Djurgården, the Royal National Park in Stockholm, and Järna, south of Stockholm (cut down because the trees were infected with Dutch elm disease). The contrast of the controlled shape of the timber and its uncontrolled structure is important to us. Just like in legendary Swedish director Ingmar Bergman's films, which are also an inspiration for Aesop, the drama lies in the contrast between the suppressed inner forces of the characters and the control of social conventions and relations to others.The massive, simply hewn forms provide a textural contrast to the smooth beige plaster wall and timber floor, walls and ceiling. The plaster wall has a warm, light beige color, like a Stockholm earth tone. The interior details in copper and leather will age beautifully together with the elm and the oak, and the patina of time and use will bring the materials even closer to each other. (2014)

(opposite page)
Early sketch.
Presentation model of sequence of spaces.

A 100-year-old elm tree trunk serving as the centerpiece of the space.

Local Context The first Aesop store in Scandinavia is situated on a side street off Biblioteksgatan, in a building in central Stockholm that was one of architects Backström & Reinius's last projects. It is an office building from 1980 with some stores on street level: a bank, an Italian coffee shop and now the first Aesop store. How did we interpret Stockholm and the Nordic? One of the references given by our client was the film tradition of Ingmar Bergman. This allowed us to turn to a heavier, deeper and more complex quality, avoiding the Nordic light approach. The Paris Aesop team were inspired by the natural Scandinavian look, which ages gracefully and beautifully. This gave us inspiration to work with a material we knew well, and which also ages beautifully and naturally: solid elm wood. From the massive trunks we shaped the three focus objects: the point of sale, the demonstration sink and the bench. Further materials in the palette were oak, copper, leather and handblown glass.

A sequence of spaces.

(opposite page left)
Aesop Bibliotekstan,
plan 1:100.

(opposite page right)
Working on elm pieces with artist Lies-Marie Hoffmann in her outdoor workshop in Gustavsberg.

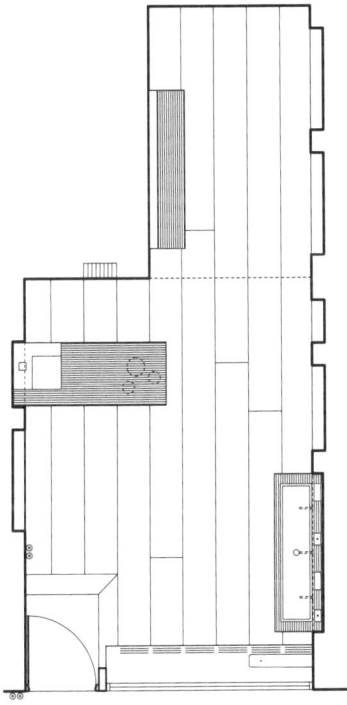

Copper Oak Elm Copper has been used for water pipes for as long as we have had running water. It does not react with water but it does with oxygen. The oxidation lends a certain character to the surface. Copper is a pure natural metal and can be reused. This made it possible for the plumber to shape a metal sheet to fit into the wooden basin and form an inner copper sink.

Oak is a very hard and durable material. When working on the Aesop store we learned a lot in dialogue with the producer of the wide wooden planks we used to form the floor, walls, shelves and ceiling. In order to achieve wider planks with less wastage, cracks were filled in and a butterfly detail added to keep the cracks together — to us this was an inspired solution, as well as a good experience of an aesthetic attitude that is respectful of the inherent qualities of the material.

When it comes to elm trees, the annual rings of larger trees are often shaped like flowers. When cut it gives a vivid pattern in cross-section. The wood itself, especially of larger trees, also has a great variety in color — when wet or oiled it is a warm yellow-brown that can shift from red to green in different parts of the same tree. In order to let the pattern and character of the wood show through, we deliberately worked with very simple geometries to form the wooden objects. Working with these massive pieces of wood, we had to consider the distortion that would take place over time as the timber slowly dried. Butterfly joints, darkened with ammonia, were placed to hold them together, and, like at Elma, we treated the elm in the Aesop store with the French Le Tonkinois oil, which is a treatment that has to be renewed over time. The elm pieces were created in collaboration with wood artist Lies-Marie Hoffmann.

Aesop SoFo

The character of the SoFo area in Stockholm is informal and intimate and we wanted to bring that atmosphere into the design of the Aesop SoFo store. The building on Nytorgsgatan where the store is located was built in the 1950s, again designed by some of our favourite architects, Backström & Reinius. It is a remarkable building that we had studied before and it became a strong departure point for our design. The building is well maintained, with many original details still intact, including the floor and the teak interiors of the entrance. The space is very small but high-ceilinged and we wanted it to be open and inviting, like a domestic living room. Inspired by the way the architect Gunnar Asplund used bent wood in a functionally and spatially defining manner at the Woodland Cemetery chapels, we used a 0.7 millimeter veneer as drapery to wrap and unify a space interrupted by pillars and a stair volume. The verticality of the geometry amplifies the height of the space and, just like a curtain, the play of light and shadow gives the materiality and color very tactile and subtle qualities. The veneer is of alder wood, chosen for its warm color and its calm, unified character, and to match the existing teak on the facade and in the entrance area. The alder veneer of the walls is paired with solid alder wood in details where needed for purposes of durability, construction or an appearance of solidity. The lower, continuous wooden divider transforms in relation to the different areas to create display shelves, a door handle or just a horizontal line that ties the geometry together. The brass shelves for product display are slightly patinated. The existing concrete floor, hidden for eighty years under layers of tiles, was ground to a smooth but still rough surface, so that the aggregate becomes visible, massive in contrast to the lightness of the veneer. The ceiling is painted a pink-beige color to match the veneer but lighter, to achieve a contrast with the walls and show the shape of the space in relation to the ceiling, where it is readable as a whole. The leather of the bench is vegetable-tanned and will age beautifully. (2016)

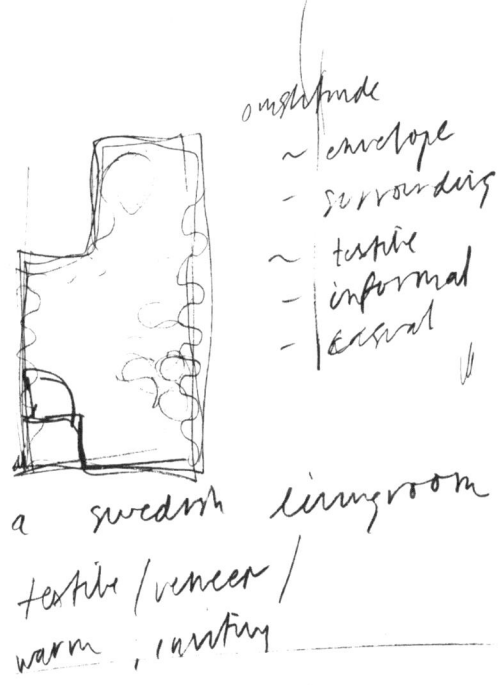

Asplund For inspiration we visited the Gunnar Asplund's Woodland Cemetery in Stockholm together with our client, and the waiting rooms of the chapels became an important starting point for Aesop SoFo. In these rooms, material and space are one, as the wooden veneer wall transforms into a bench. It is a spatial way of working with wooden veneer, and we took the opportunity to study its inherent quality of only being able to be bent in one direction. We also turned to Bruno Mathsson, the Swedish master of bent wood, to study his technique of creating soft shapes from hard wood. His modernist, light interiors with a rich materiality make for warm, enclosing spaces with an informal character.

(opposite page)
A seating niche in the back,
a place to sit down and rest.

(left)
Early sketch of veneer
wrapping the space.

(right)
Inspiration for the client and us:
the waiting rooms of the Woodland
Cemetery chapels by Gunnar
Asplund, 1940.

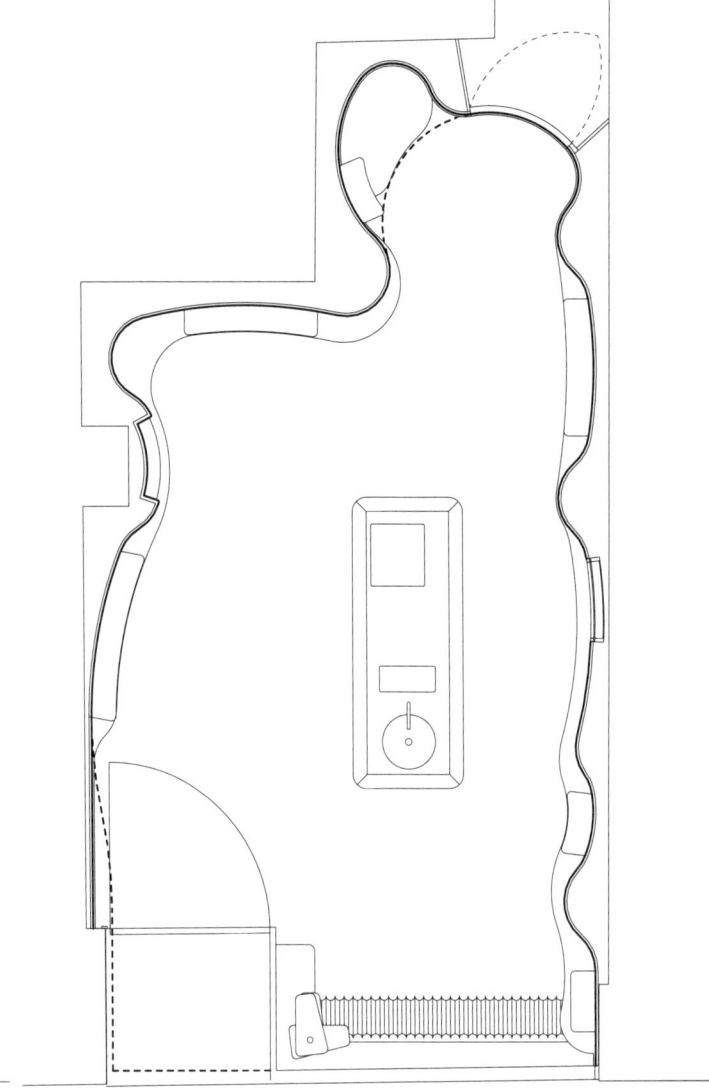

The centerpiece In contrast to the complex geometry of the surrounding walls, the shape of the centerpiece, with the point of sale area and demonstration sink, is austere and simple but softened by rounded corners in plan and in section—this detail relates to the rounded corners of the frame around the glass in the original entrance door. The lower part is made of veneer, while the walls and the top are of solid alder for a sturdier feel. The sink recessed in the top is a vintage piece made of enameled metal.

Handcrafted objects To further enhance the cozy domestic atmosphere and to reflect the handicraft tradition of the area, we sourced some high-quality design elements and handcrafted furniture. The vintage lamp and chair are accompanied by a contemporary handicraft object, a vase in black glass specially blown for this project by Simon Klenell.

Geometry In relation to production and architecture, we reduced the number of different radiuses in the space to three. The three radiuses and the individual lengths of each curve became our parameters to close the line. In a space with a shape that is hard to grasp, the repetition of the radiuses provides calm, unity and readability.

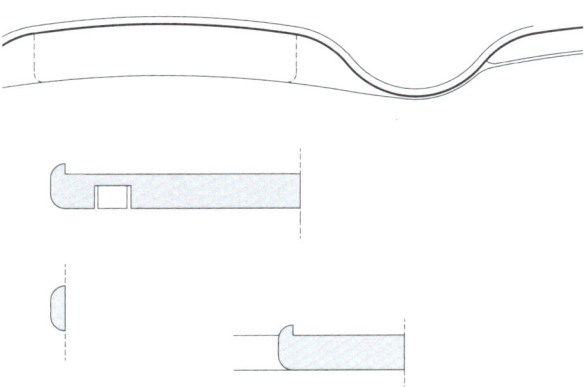

(opposite page)
Plan 1:50.

(left)
Detail of the horizontal divider
transforming from line to shelf
to handle on its way around the
space 1:5/1:25.

(right)
A view of the space with its
softly curved transitions created
by a set of three different radiuses.

Sauna Grytnäs

The mounting of the numbered logs that had already been test-mounted at the producer's workshop.

Sauna Grytnäs was built on eight concrete plinths as a contemporary log timber structure. It provided the opportunity to learn more about a building technique with a very long tradition and strong logic. In the north of Sweden, houses have been built in this tradition for centuries, and many examples are still standing, often aged naturally to a light silver-gray. In a log structure the horizontal logs are interlocked at the corners by knots, and we chose a knot with a clear-cut profile aligned with the facade for a sharp form but with the knots still exposed, marking the corners and the position of the inner walls. The possible lengths of the logs and the positioning of the joints were parameters that we learned to work with in dialogue with the producer. The foundation plinths have to meet the knots. A log structure of this size sinks approximately 5 centimeters over time, and window and door details have to be adapted to this movement. The whole timber structure was first built inside a production hall before being transported and assembled on site. It has sedum on the roof and a silicate-treated facade that will turn gray over time. (2021)

Entrance veranda — the foundations consist of eight concrete plinths reaching down to solid rock 2 meters below ground.

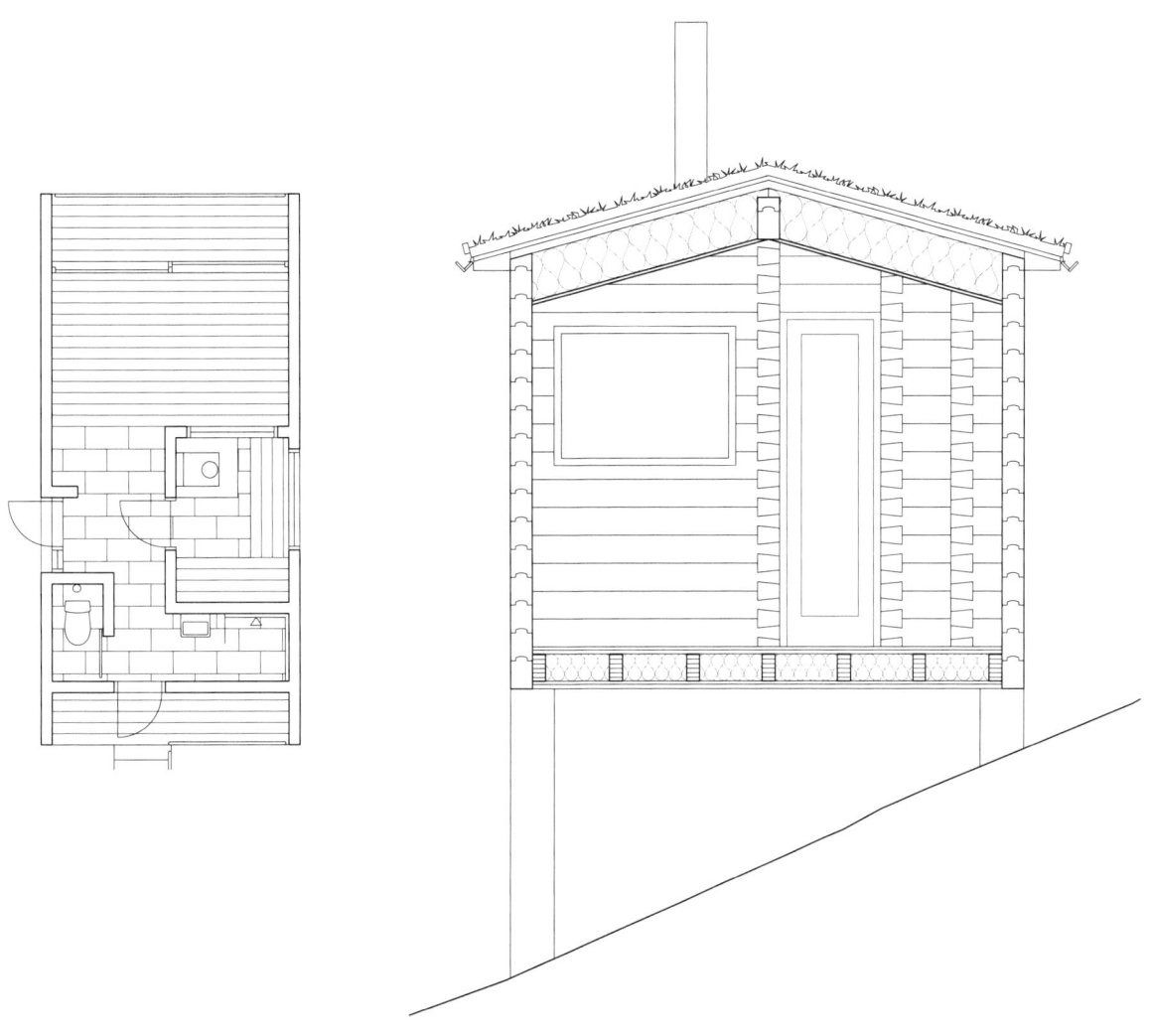

(opposite page)
A view through the log timber house.

(left)
Plan 1:100.
(right)
Section 1:50.

Artbarn

Artbarn is a studio added to a farmstead in Roslagen. The grandfather in the family was an art lover and collector and the space needed a lot of wall space and light from the north. Owing to the historic context as well as the building's function as an art gallery, the typology that was deemed suitable was that of a barn. A site was chosen at a slight distance from the main house, to ensure that the new studio would become a retreat with its own view over meadows and fields. The interior has an exposed CLT massive wood construction that was painted with linseed oil paint and a polished and oiled concrete floor. Cut-outs from the walls were used for doors and benches. The roof is made of Rheinzink, and Roslagen tar was used for the facade treatment. The carefully positioned rooflights provide northerly light and leave the walls free for the hanging of art. The barn doors close the house, as well as blocking out direct sunlight to preserve the artworks. (2014)

CO_2 Cross-laminated timber has the valuable property of storing CO_2, which is a very important parameter in the development of a sustainable building industry. The construction method has great potential for architectural qualities, which we have explored with enthusiasm. Considering that the Artbarn was our first house in CLT, we are grateful to have had a client who understood the challenges and allowed us to start investigating this construction system.

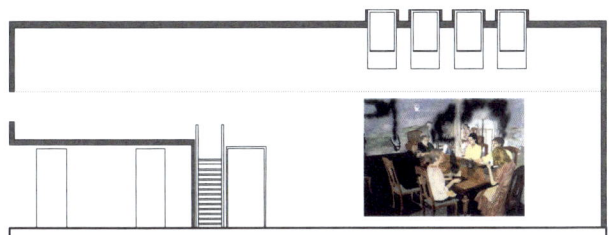

(opposite page)
Interior view of gallery space.

(top to bottom)
Mounting of the CLT roof boards cut to interlock each other.

Exterior view.

(left)
Section showing the spatial idea 1:400.

Tree House

Tree House is part of the urbanization and densification of Hallonbergen Centrum in Sundbyberg. The project was developed in a regulation plan with distinct limitations regarding footprint and height and had to be conceived within the given framework. The volumes were formed as an intermediary between the neighboring 1970s lamella housing and the new tower houses. We designed them as a link between the two—the gables forming a dialogue with the verticality of the neighboring recent tower blocks, and the rhythm of the long facades harmonizing with the historic lamella housing.

The site slopes steeply toward the north, and the entrance facade to the south faces a local street as part of its densification, in order to give it a more urban character. The south facade provides very good sunlight, the open situation to the north offers long views, and to the west the apartments have views toward a wooded area. The apartments are planned to profit from the different positions, and the larger apartments have windows in two or three directions. The facade material follows the logic of the construction: since the two lower floors, which are partly underground, will be built in concrete they will have a concrete facade, while the eight upper stories with a structure of CLT wood have a wooden facade. The wooden facade is smooth and plain, providing a backdrop to the rhythm of the windows and balconies. The window placement is kept repetitive and simple, while the grouping of balconies and variation in balcony fronts creates a layered rhythm that breaks down the scale of the volumes. The two volumes have a slight difference in color—brown and black. As a contrast to the facade, the windows, the eaves and the facade partitions around entrances are painted in a contrasting ochre. The project includes 140 apartments, a commercial space along the street, a common outdoor area and a parking garage, and it has a total area of approximately 14,100 square meters over ten stories. The CLT for the load-bearing structure is in the facades, the cores, the inner lengthwise walls and some partition walls, creating a rather strict grid complemented with lighter walls to form the layout. (2020–ongoing)

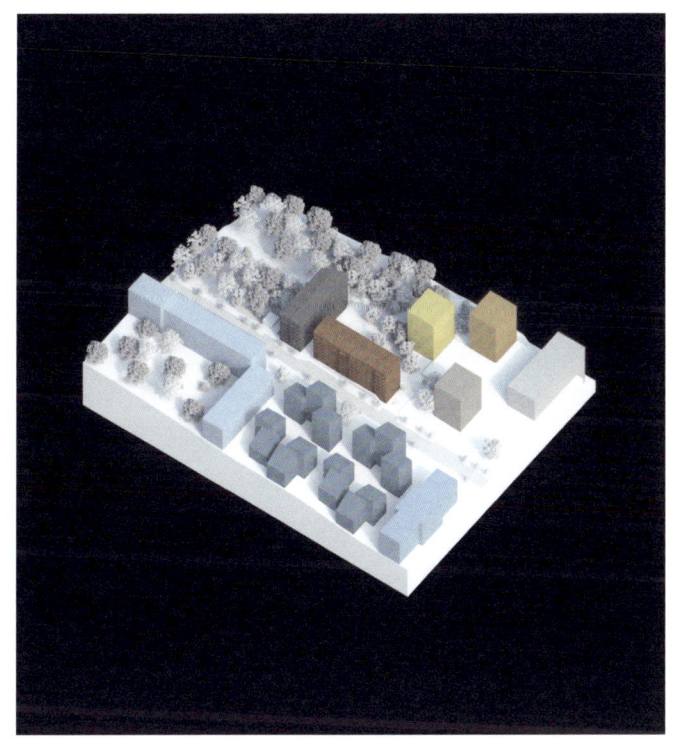 

Facade The facade in a smooth wooden paneling is fire-protected and colored dark gray and brown. The treatment, which also ensures durability over time, is achieved through a heating process in chamber kilns. The concrete of the lower floors and supporting walls is cast on site as a prefabricated element on wooden paneled walls to obtain an imprint that works in dialogue with the wooden facade.

(opposite page)
View of entrance area.

(left)
Color concept in contextual axonometric view.

(right)
Tree House street view.

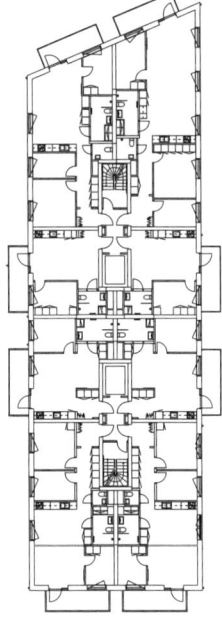
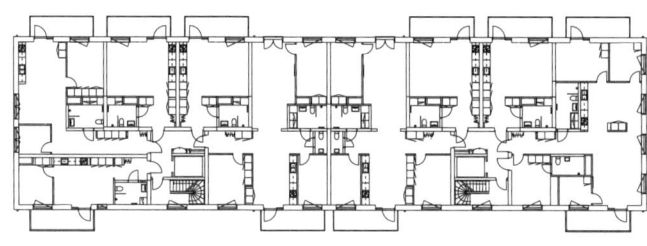

Typical floorplan 1:600.

Framing Space

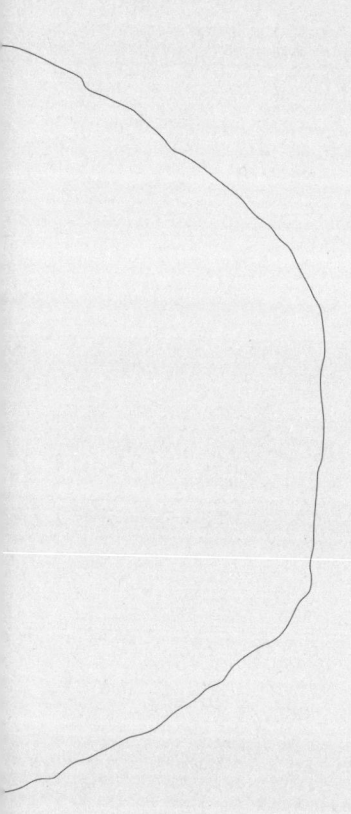

Solbrinken

The Solbrinken houses serve as a home with a connecting studio for a large family and their friends, where work and leisure time overlap. A creative space for a designer of sporting apparel, and a photographer and carpenter, the houses are situated in the woods between an old garden and wild pine trees. The foundation is made from a concrete slab polished to create the perfect indoor floor for skateboarding. The main house has a high, horizontal space for everyday living, including the kitchen and social space. The entrance floor has a direct connection to the nature outside and three sleeping cabins, one for each of the youths in the family. In the loft there is a larger main bedroom as well as an extra space, which can be changed and turned around over time. It also has a generous bathroom and a separate room with a shower. The kitchen is placed in the part of the house that has the highest ceiling, with a central core that creates a focal point in the large open space. A separate workroom or bedroom is placed next to the kitchen. The studio is situated on the other side of the connecting courtyard, which features casual landscaping.

Diagonal concrete walls handle the height differences of the site, creating informal seating on a white gravel surface. The two volumes are placed slightly at an angle to each other to add dynamism to the outer spaces. In relief, the black-painted facade has a textile-like effect with variation created through shadows. (2009)

(previous spread)
The entrance between the two volumes.

Interregnum, a space in between For us, finding a campsite, a shore to anchor by or *where to put your hat* is the starting point of architecture. Creating a new space in an existing landscape is a challenge for every architect and for us the beginning of a project. It is a decision that has to be made wisely, with respect for natural and cultural sustainability. We see it as creating an in-between space — an interregnum — relating to the inside and the outside, and to objects in the surrounding nature.

In this case, the site and a personal experience the client had on the site were the starting points for the project. We were keen to make the most of the large oak trees and other valuable natural qualities of the site and let them become an integrated part of the project. On one of the client's first visits they saw two majestic ravens land here — an experience that became a metaphor for the project, creating a story as well as a design direction.

(opposite page)
A raven in his black shining feather suit.

The studio is sunk into the ground.

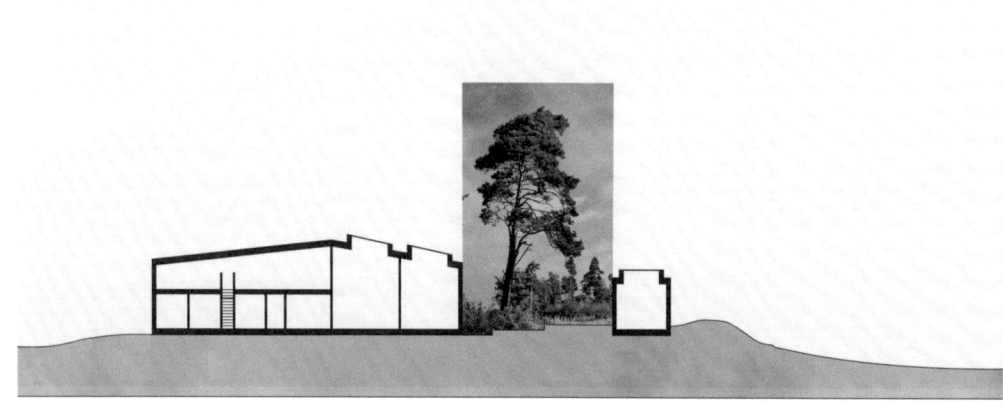

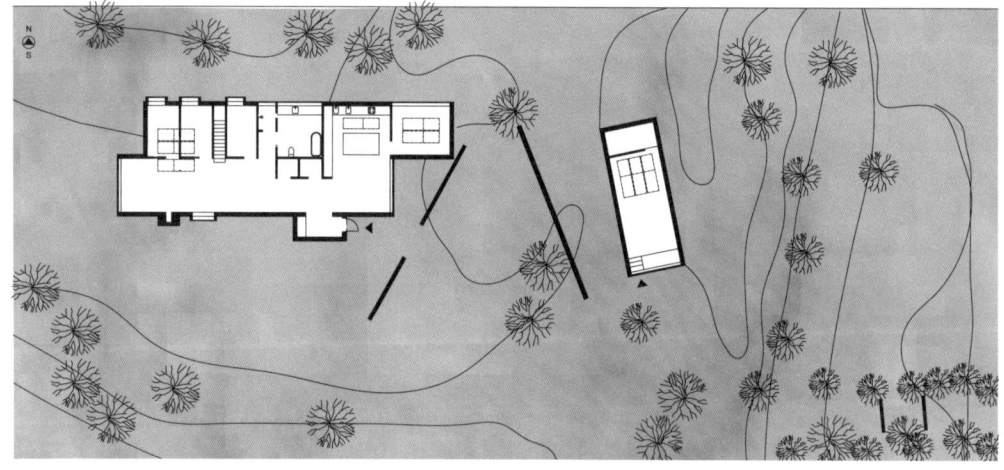

Section and plan showing the
space between the volumes 1:400.

(opposite page)
A living room for skateboarding and
working, facing the untouched forest.

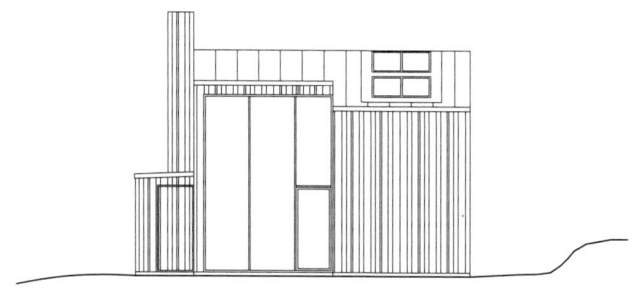
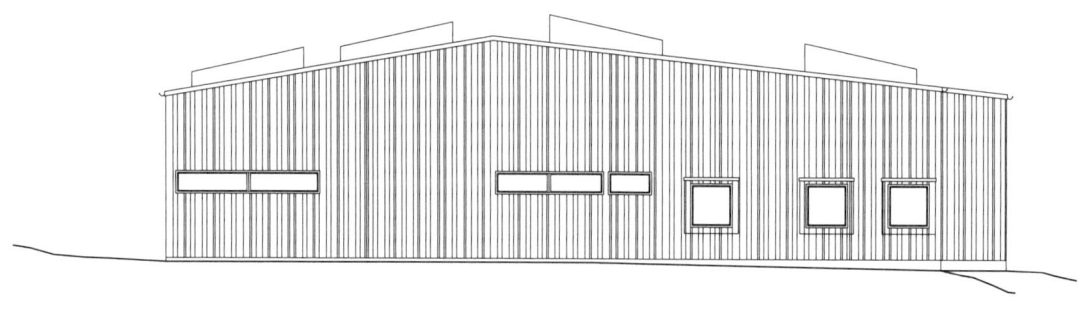

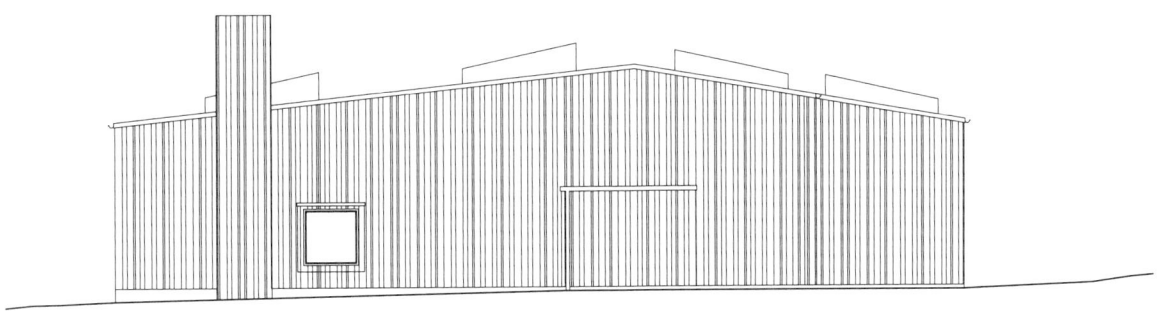
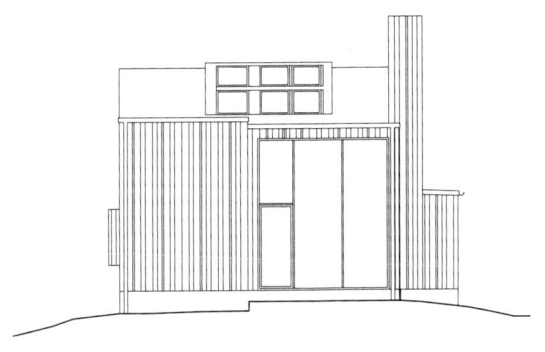

Facades 1:200.

(opposite page)
The high vertical kitchen space.

(left)
The spatial connection between the kitchen and the living room with upper spaces.

(right)
Interregnum, the space between the buildings.

Risön Cabin

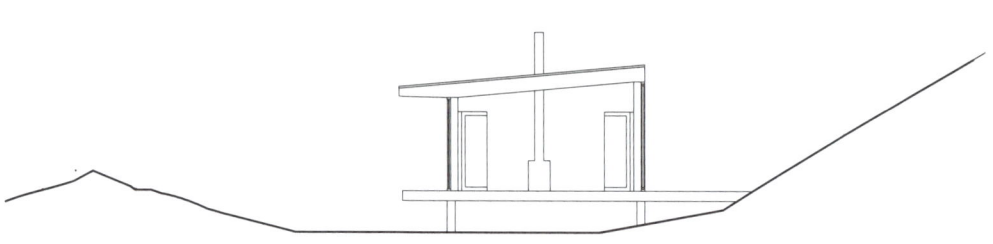

Risön Cabin was planned for a young family with two children on one of the last unbuilt sites on a small island in the archipelago off the Swedish west coast. The client wanted a simple house and we sought inspiration in the Swedish 1960s and 1970s tradition of sports cabins—a typology with a simple building volume, including a combined kitchen and living room and small bedrooms, planned for shorter vacation stays by the sea, in the forest or in the mountains. The site provided views of the sea to the north and a dramatic cliff to the south, and the volume was placed to create a wind-protected outdoor area to the south. With generous windows in the main space opening up the house on two sides, sea views could be offered throughout. The roof was angled to let the sun inside and with an overhang toward the sea to create a protected outdoor area.

The house was built on site by the island's local carpenter using a wooden balloon frame structure. Since the site is situated very low, the house had to be raised on plinths both in order to take advantage of the view and as a precaution against rising sea levels and storm water.

The substructure with high glued laminated timber (glulam) beams is shielded by the cliffs and has a generous staircase toward the water. The facade is painted in a warm light gray with contrasting darker window frames. The interior has a wooden floor, and the ceiling and walls of the larger room have wooden panels stained in white. The bedrooms feature contrasting wallpaper for intimacy. (2016)

(previous spread left)
View from the sea.
Section 1:200.
(previous spread right)
View through the building.

(above)
Terrace toward the sea.

Living room connecting
to outdoor spaces.

In Praise of Loos Loft

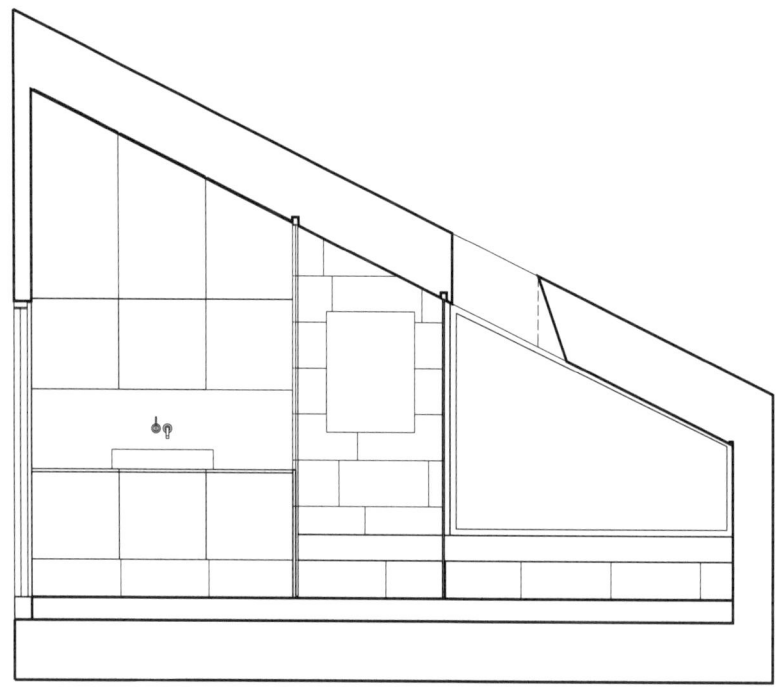

We were approached by a couple who really liked the apartment they lived in and wanted it to be extended with a terrace and a new bathroom with a steam sauna. The aim was to create a home where the clients—owners of one of the best rock clubs in Stockholm—could relax and recharge their batteries, as well as entertain friends in a private, more intimate context. For the layout we sought inspiration in Adolf Loos's Raumplan concept and the materiality in his very intimate interior spaces. Diagonal sightlines between indoor and outdoor spaces tie them together into a larger whole, extending the space out over the surrounding roofscape. The terrace is generously glazed and fitted with sliding doors to become an integrated part of the apartment. The bathroom is divided into a dry zone where all wall and roof surfaces are clad in walnut veneer, and a limestone-clad wet zone, maximizing the use of the available section. (2013)

(opposite page)
Section 1:50.

A bathroom and steam sauna
with a private view onto the terrace.

(following spread)
View from the sauna overlooking
the terrace.

Guldboda

Guldboda posed a challenge for the architects, Katarina Lundeberg and Petra Gipp. The clients were a couple with different ideas: one wanted to be in the dark and the other in the sun. They envisioned living in the archipelago close to nature and in an interplay between privacy and transparency. The house faces the water, closed to the north and open with a view to the west. The two distinct volumes take hold of each other and allow light from above to divide the space. One has cells for sleeping with direct access to the exterior, a bedroom with a terrace and a bathroom that opens up to the sky. The other volume consists of a combined living room and kitchen open to the view and terrace. We wanted to leave the site as unharmed as possible, visually as well as conceptually. Materials and details were chosen with care to emphasize the architectonic whole and so they would age with dignity. Exterior wood panels were coated with iron vitriol and corners were mitered. Site-cast concrete was used along with details in sheet zinc, and a plinth foundation raises the house above the ground, leaving the site virtually untouched. (2009)

Entrance facade offering a view through the building.

(opposite page)
Framed view from the entrance, looking out over the sea where the rock drops down steeply.

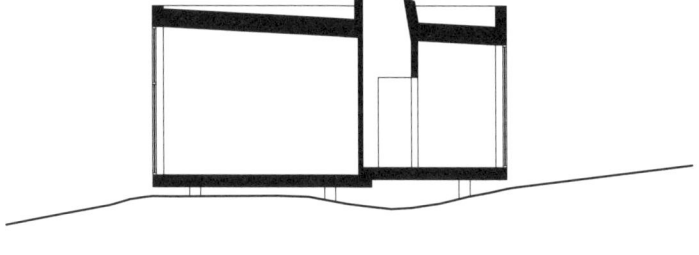

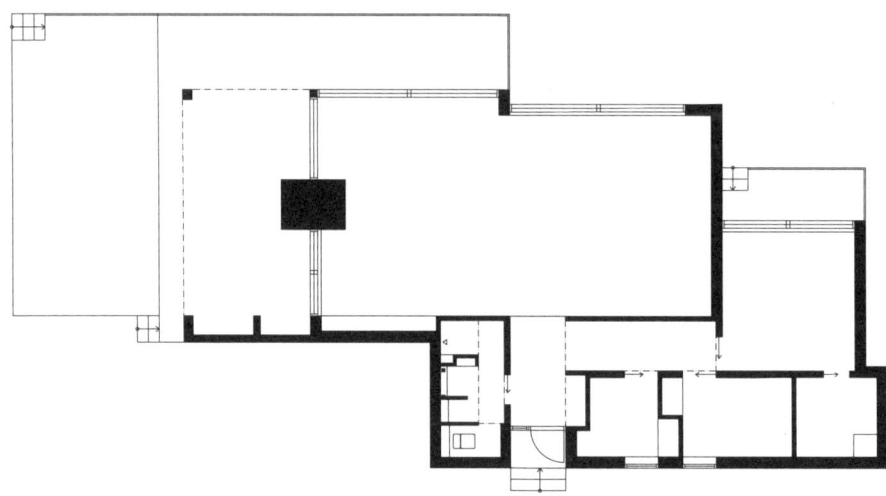

(above)
Section and plan 1:400.
(below)
Casa Malaparte,
Adalberto Libera, 1937.

Building on a rock After seeing the site and starting to envision a building at the site, our thoughts went directly to the much-admired Casa Malaparte in Capri by Adalberto Libera. The iconic building has a life of its own through films, photos and a number of publications, and we have in fact once stood outside its gates. Like others, we are fascinated by the concentrated framed views, which give character to the space, and the "stairs to heaven" that integrate the building with its site.

Side facade with stairs to the roof. A building with a strong appearance if you pass by boat.

Storön

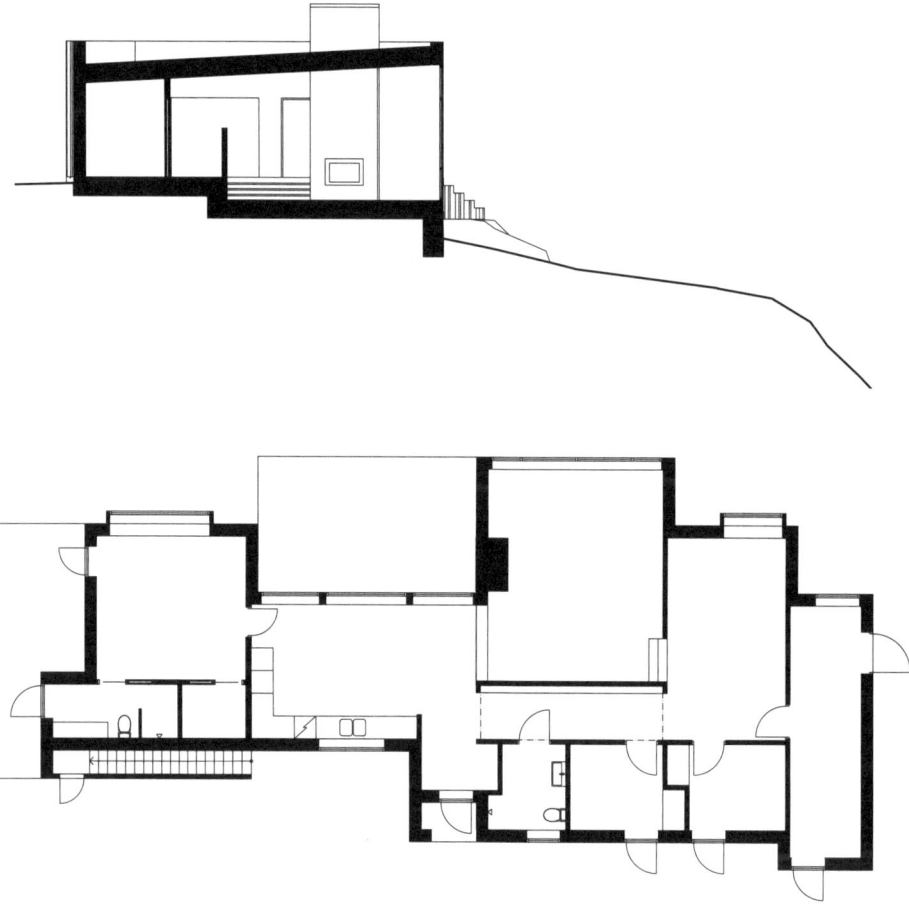

In designing the Storön house, on a cliff in the northern Stockholm archipelago, we were inspired by the former house on the site, which followed the cliff formation and was divided into smaller volumes. It is designed as a place to live and work and with generous common spaces for a big family with friends. There is a private writing space in the north for the author in the family and a private master bedroom in the south toward the blueberry fields. Guests have their own doors leading directly out into the morning sun. The shifts in level create a number of wind-protected outdoor areas on all sides of the house. The house is made of prefabricated wooden wall elements acquired from a local carpenter. The interior cladding and the facade are made of panels with varying widths, painted white inside and treated with iron vitriol on the exterior to turn gray over time. The foundation is made of concrete formed in situ, following the rocks and precisely meeting the different levels of the upper facade. (2015)

The volume shifts in relation to the cliff and thus has a spatial quality both inside and to the exterior. Section and plan 1:200

The wooden structure of the terrace, under roof and pergola, cut to meet the rock.

Frames and views It is a privilege and a challenge to work with interested clients and their dreams for a new home, transforming their thoughts and vision into physical form. Functionality is a task to solve in a more programmatic manner, but spatial experiences and expression take longer to define. In this project we talked about different framed views and also specifically about how they were to be framed — if they should be divided or just seen through a single large glass pane. Here we decided on a divided window as an interpretation of the archipelago glass veranda from the time around the turn of the nineteenth century, but on a different scale, finding a balance between enclosing window bars and large glass areas bringing in the view.

The lower living room has a subdivided window pushed forward to gain a clear view over the landscape.

View from the kitchen
and the pergola.

A window of one's own to sit in.

A precise meeting of the wooden facade and the concrete base of the recessing volumes. Beautiful craftsmanship by the local builder at Blidö, Eric T.

KIKA Landsort

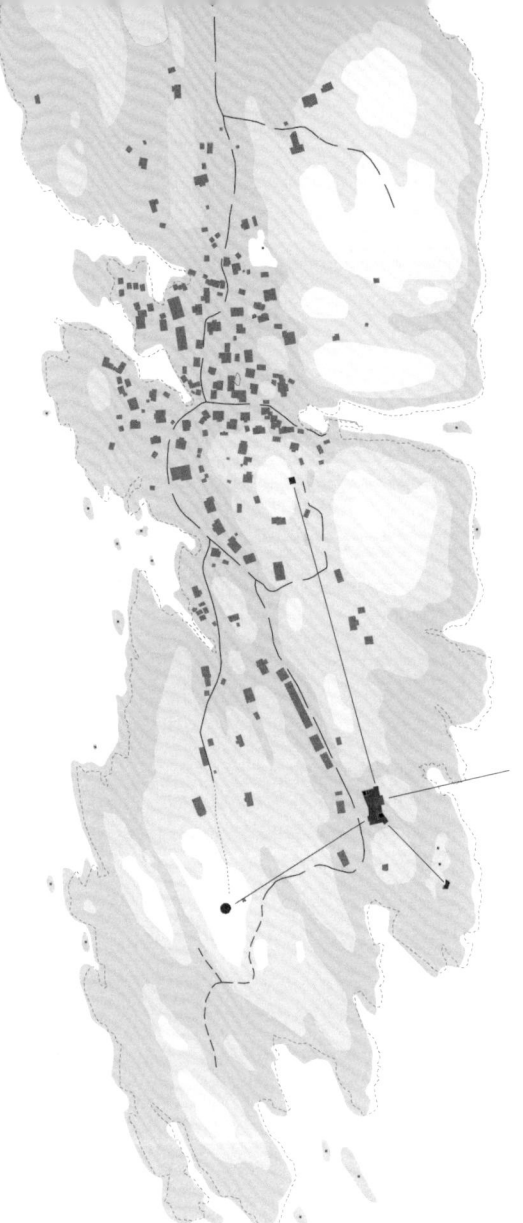

The island of Öja is the outpost farthest south of the Stockholm–Nynäshamn–Södertälje archipelago. It is a pilot station with a long tradition of supporting the southern access of cargo ships to Stockholm and beyond via Lake Mälaren. The small village of Landsort on the southern tip of Öja is where the pilot boats set off to guide ships through the rocky archipelago. It used to be a village with a school, but now permanent residents are very few while the population multiplies during the summer. The military has left the island but there are still some good restaurants, a hotel, a youth hostel, a bird research center and a church, but nowhere indoors for visitors to shelter or seek information.

The KIKA project was commissioned by a local organization that asked us to create a building that would act as a node for the continued evolution of Landsort, and make it a more attractive place for year-round living in the archipelago. The building was to make the Baltic maritime heritage visible and accessible on a site where it originated, and provide an understanding of the Baltic Sea context from a historic as well as a contemporary perspective. Furthermore, the building was to become the visitors' portal to the sights at Landsort, hosting exhibitions for tourists to be inspired by, for students to learn from and for researchers to develop knowledge further, as well as a place for locals to gather. The historic buildings on Öja—the older lighthouse, the newer concrete pilot tower, as well as the bunkers and fishermen's and pilots' houses—were all built in a pragmatic manner according to their required function, as well as the technical possibilities and building methods available at the time of construction. When given the task of designing a building in this context, in very harsh conditions where all buildings are totally exposed, we chose to work with the same attitude. Climate change is one of the main issues of contemporary society, including the building industry, hence to build in our times means to take this question into account. In line with this thinking, we designed KIKA as a CLT structure clad in a wooden facade and with the possibility to use solar energy as well as heat from the rock below. (2014)

(opposite page)
Site plan 1:7500. The island of Öja with its soft rocks shaped by inland ice and its focus point, Landsort, between the east and west harbors. KIKA placed south of the settlement, taking in viewpoints in all four directions.

View from the north. Walking to the southern tip, after passing former marine barracks that are now a hostel, one arrives at a gravel site that is the site of our proposal for the KIKA Landsort meeting place for maritime heritage.

KIKA, which in its essence is about displaying Öja, is designed like a looking machine, with an interior that frames views in all four directions onto the landscape and the adjacent iconic buildings. To the west is the lighthouse, to the north the pilot tower, to the south a bunker and to the east the Baltic Sea, which connects us to our neighbors across the water and which has played an important part in the history of the island. The overall volume and its direction relate to the direction of the Öja cliffs, created when they were shaped by inland ice a very long time ago. In addition to this, the cliffs have cracked perpendicular to their main direction and the island, providing another direction for us to consider when forming the building. The building relates to the site and exterior experiences but also gives an inner experience of the strong Nordic light through skylights and provides the visitor with a walk through an exhibition that is made up of a variety of visual experiences, objects and information.

A view toward the lighthouse.

(opposite page)
Elevations of KIKA Landsort, 1:500.
The building is adjusted to meet the rock formations.

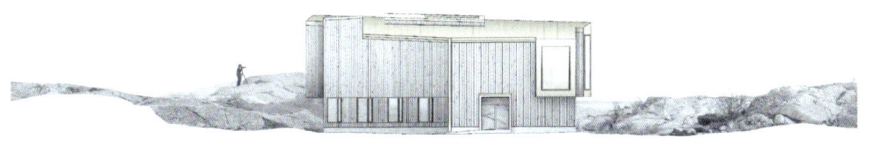

Magelungens Strand

Magelungens Strand, south of Stockholm, is part of a new regional plan for Farsta with the aim to connect the area to neighboring Fagersjö. A spin-off from Klockelund, with the same ambition to provide new housing in wood with generous balconies, it is a project formed from two different scales. To the north, along the main road Magelungsvägen, the strategy has been to break down the volume, creating two "towers" in dialogue with the existing tower blocks in the neighborhood, and to work with additional detailing on street level to create an attractive street front. To the south, where the houses and all apartments face a large landscaped space opening up over Magelungen Lake, we have instead used the expressive balcony structure to tie the volume together, giving it a unified, solitary character. The diagonals of the balconies are structural and they add a "knitted" textile feel, wrapping around the volumes as a whole. The building is beautifully situated and the surrounding nature is made accessible via a local pedestrian walkway and bike path that will also serve as the access road. The shoreline has a rich biodiversity of birds, bats and insects and to support these we have integrated nests for birds and bats, and hives for bees in the balcony structure. The land around the buildings will be left untouched, while barbecuing areas for the inhabitants and smaller playgrounds will be sparsely distributed in a number of circular areas. There are additional green areas on the roof, including a common greenhouse and a roof terrace for gardening and social interaction. (2016–ongoing)

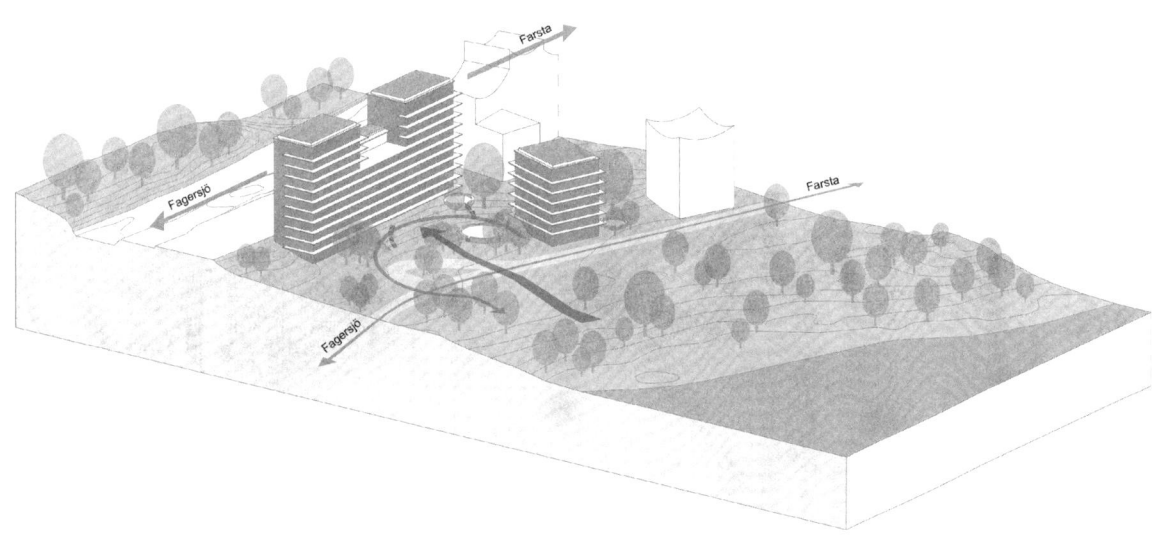

(opposite page)
In the shorter perspective of the street view the volume is divided in two.

Conceptual axonometric view.

The filigree balcony structure provides generous spaces as well as an overall unified volume facing the large landscape, with the lake Magelungen and the forests behind.

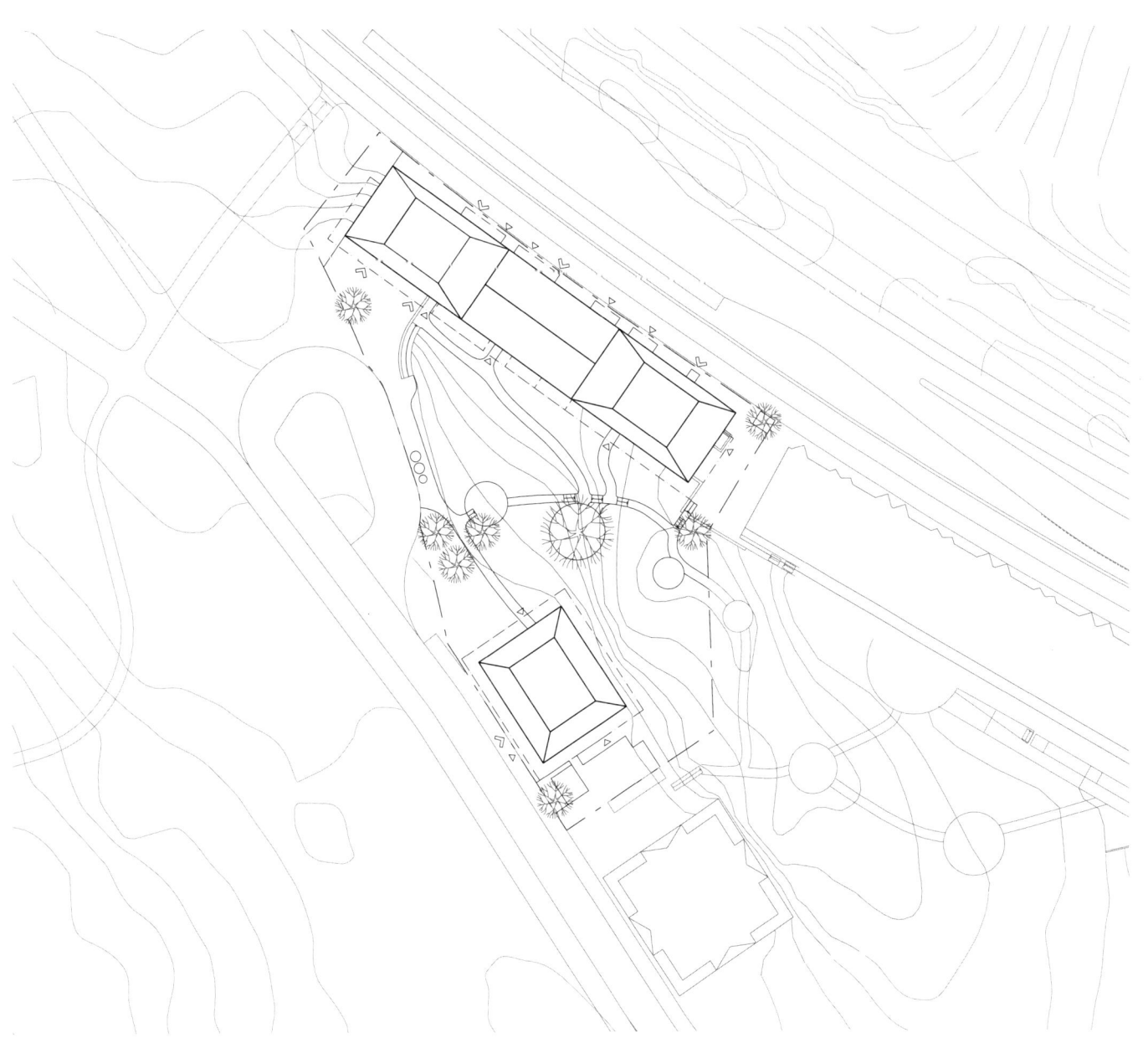

The landscape is planned as "restored nature" with smaller circular areas for garden life. A shared roof terrace sits between the higher parts of the building toward the street, facing the sun and the view of the lake. 1:1000.

Vega

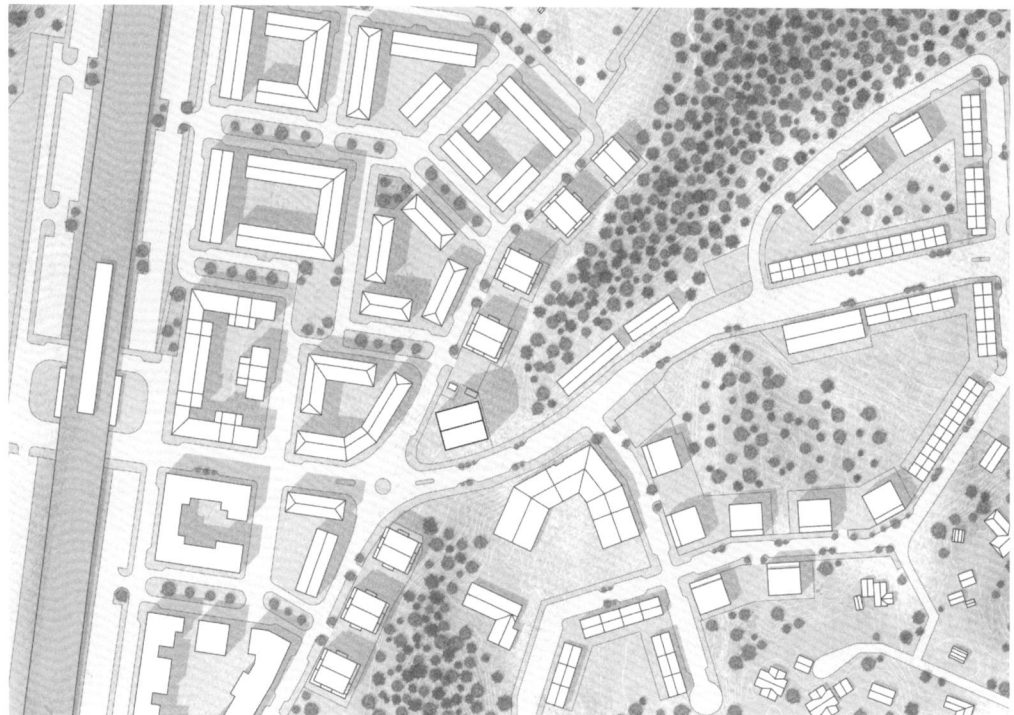

Vegastaden developed out of the rather unique opportunity to open up a new commuter train station along an existing route. The train line connects Stockholm with Nynäshamn, and the Haninge municipality took the opportunity to plan a new suburb of approximately 3,500 homes for 10,000 inhabitants around the new station. Our client has many building rights in this area and the blocks Horisont, Nadir and Zenit are the first to be finished. The projects were developed within a given regulation plan that defined the buildings in volume but gave us free rein when it came to aesthetics. The three blocks are the first in a row of eight that will provide a backdrop for the settlement as a whole. The volumes are shaped with a pitched roof, providing a characteristic silhouette toward the street. There is a wide range of floor plans, including apartments of different sizes where all but the smallest ones have the common areas placed in a corner with generous balconies formed to be part of the volume. The large windows provide light and offer views, and the placement is unified and repetitive in order to create a calm overall character.

The facade is of metal cassettes in aluminum zinc-plated steel, a material that shifts in character in relation to the time of day and the weather, and that will age beautifully. As a contrast, the window frames are painted yellow, and to provide an attractive street front, the facade of the entrance level is clad with wooden ribs that continue up to cover the surface of the over-hanging roof. The generous entrance hall also provides views to the back entrance and gets its austere character from the exposed concrete of the structure. (2020)

Materiality We let the materials remain visible as much as possible, to be honest and not cover them merely to obscure building techniques. The concrete walls remain unadorned in the entrance halls, exposing the process of the concrete technique. The thin facade material was a result of planning with strict cost limitations, and solar panels were installed on parts of the roof.

(previous spread left)
Site plan showing Vegastaden
and the row of tower houses
along the hill to the right.

(previous spread right)
Facade of aluminum zinc-plated
steel casettes.

View from the hill behind.

Entrance view with facade
and overhanging roof clad
in thin wooden ribs.

Generous balconies with a semi-glazed railing to provide daylight and views.

Structure as Form

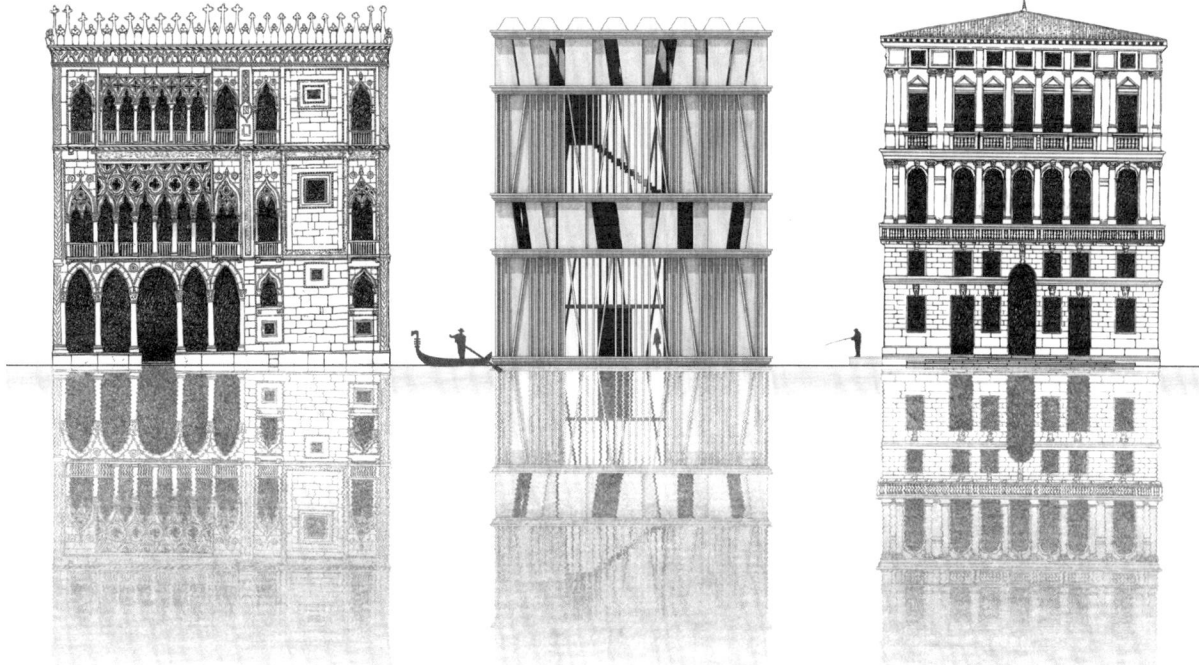

Ca d'Ombra

For the 2016 Architecture Biennale in Venice we were invited to participate in an exhibition with the theme of working with wooden architecture for a future expanded Venice. We studied the classical Ca' d'Oro and Ca' Corner della Regina — some of the finest palaces along the Grand Canal in Venice — for inspiration, and our contribution became a transformation of the classic palazzo into a wooden palazzo. This project was also transformed into a research project for our later pavilions and our ongoing housing projects in the Stockholm area. We based our design of the Palace of Shadows on two different structural systems for building in wood, CLT boards and glued laminated timber (glulam) pillar and beam structures. From these systems we created a complex spatiality with a variety of light and shadows. The facade varies between open sections with slender wooden pillars, providing great views out onto the canals and water surfaces of Venice, and more closed sections consisting of movable triangular walls made of massive wooden boards. The intense light from the strong reflections in the lagoon will be drawn from the sky lantern roof down through all the floors via the central atrium.

The inspiration for the movement through the building comes from Ca' Corner della Regina, where an intricate stair solution creates a public yet quite closed room at the entrance and you are led, via the interior balcony, up to the loggia with an open facade of pillars. In our palazzo the staircase is the building's heart, and it shifts in position around the atrium, creating a varied spatial experience. The Palace of Shadows forms the framework for a public library to be placed on the proposed additional islands in the Venetian lagoon. We chose the library as a typology since in our age it is not only a place to seek literature and information but also an informal space for social gatherings and one of the few public institutions still open to everyone regardless of their position in society. From this point of view, we feel that our library would play an important part in the New Venice as a door-opener to cultural institutions and as a contribution to the processes of democracy and integration.

(previous page)
View of Ca d'Ombra placed
in between Ca' d'Oro and
Ca' Corner della Regina.

Facade shaped from CLT
boards and glulam pillars.

Section through the spiraling
staircase in the center
of the building.

105

Loggia d'Ombra

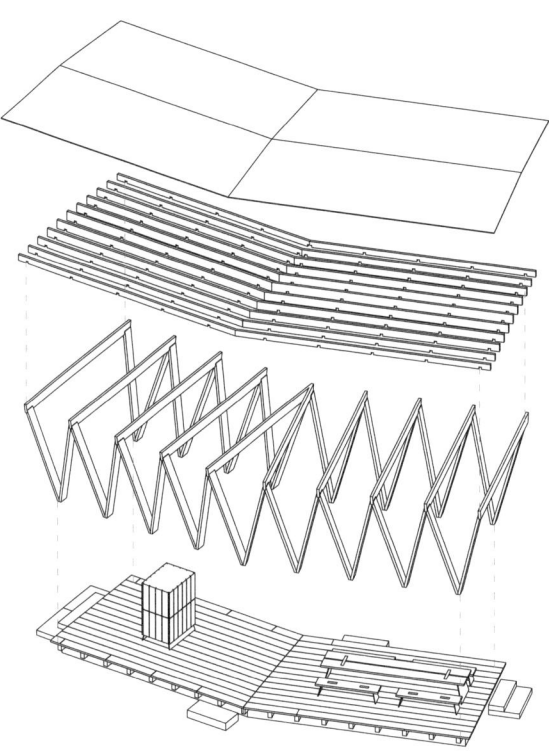

Loggia d'Ombra was a temporary wooden pavilion in the garden of Serra dei Giardini in Venice on display during the 2018 Architecture Biennale. The program prescribed an outdoor space that could act as a stage for events and a space for seminars, providing protection from the sun and rain—a transparent, open and inviting space. The task was to construct it in wood and for it to be easy to assemble and dismantle for future use. We engaged in close consultation with the glulam producer to understand and develop their mode of industrial digitally controlled production and to investigate new possible building systems. The pavilion is shaped like a loggia, adding an outdoor shaded space to the greenhouse and the garden.

Our work entered into direct dialogue with the nineteenth-century greenhouse, with its geometry as well as its function. The geometric design is tailored to catch the sun and optimize solar radiation. To form a loggia for the greenhouse, we inverted the geometry of the greenhouse plan to crate a shape that blocks the sun instead of capturing it and to allow a shaded space in front of the café.

The angle of the greenhouse fold is repeated in plan, section and elevation, creating a repetitive structure where a displacement of the module in the middle creates the fold in plan. The V-shaped columns are leaning in section, making the roof larger than the floor in order to provide shelter for the perimeter of the loggia, where the floor becomes a place to sit. A pavilion mimicking and contrasting with the greenhouse; a pavilion where the perimeter is the center.

To rationalize the production, the complex geometry focused on the leaning V-shaped columns so that all the other glulam components could be formed with a simple cut. The greenhouse of the Giardini is made of cast iron in the tradition of the crystal palaces of the era. The cast iron structure has the logic of a wooden structure, and as an inversion of this logic the wooden glulam structure of the loggia is given a thin metallic varnish. The bolts keeping it together are a reference to the traditional joining of cast iron, as well as a way to ensure rational dismantling and rebuilding. (2018)

(opposite page)
Axonometric view
of parts 1:200.

Structure in glulam with stairs of Istrian limestone, a stone traditionally used in Venice.

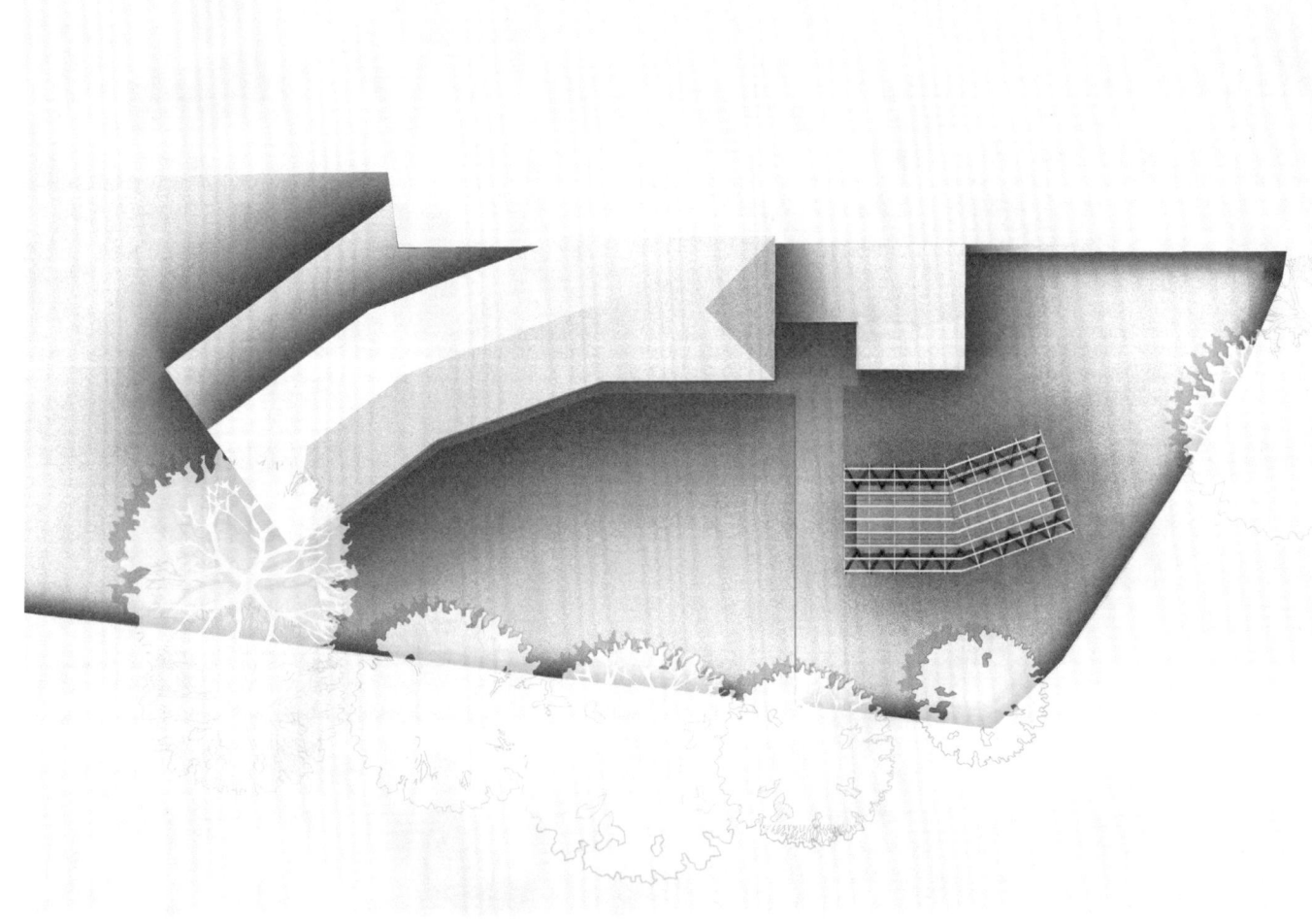

Site plan.

Researching the kinds of spaces and structures prevalent in the Italian and Swedish contexts led us to the typologies of the loggia and the traditional Swedish dance pavilion. In this context the loggia interests us as an architectural typology since it is very present in Venice. It is a private or semipublic space, basically a floor and a roof, with columns to keep them apart and create a space. The traditional Swedish dance pavilion consist of the same elements, and although they occur in very different contexts, these typologies are very similar in their structure of a floor, a roof and a transparent structure to carry the roof. They also have a similar social purpose as both provide the double function of an inner space to gather in and a perimeter that is just as important, providing the opportunity for informal interaction, viewing and being seen.

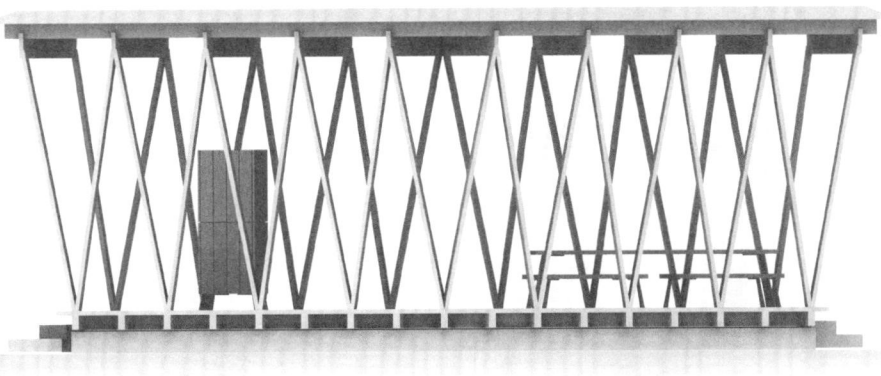

(above)
Elevation of pavilion with cabinet, bench and table 1:100.

(below)
Dansbana Forshem.

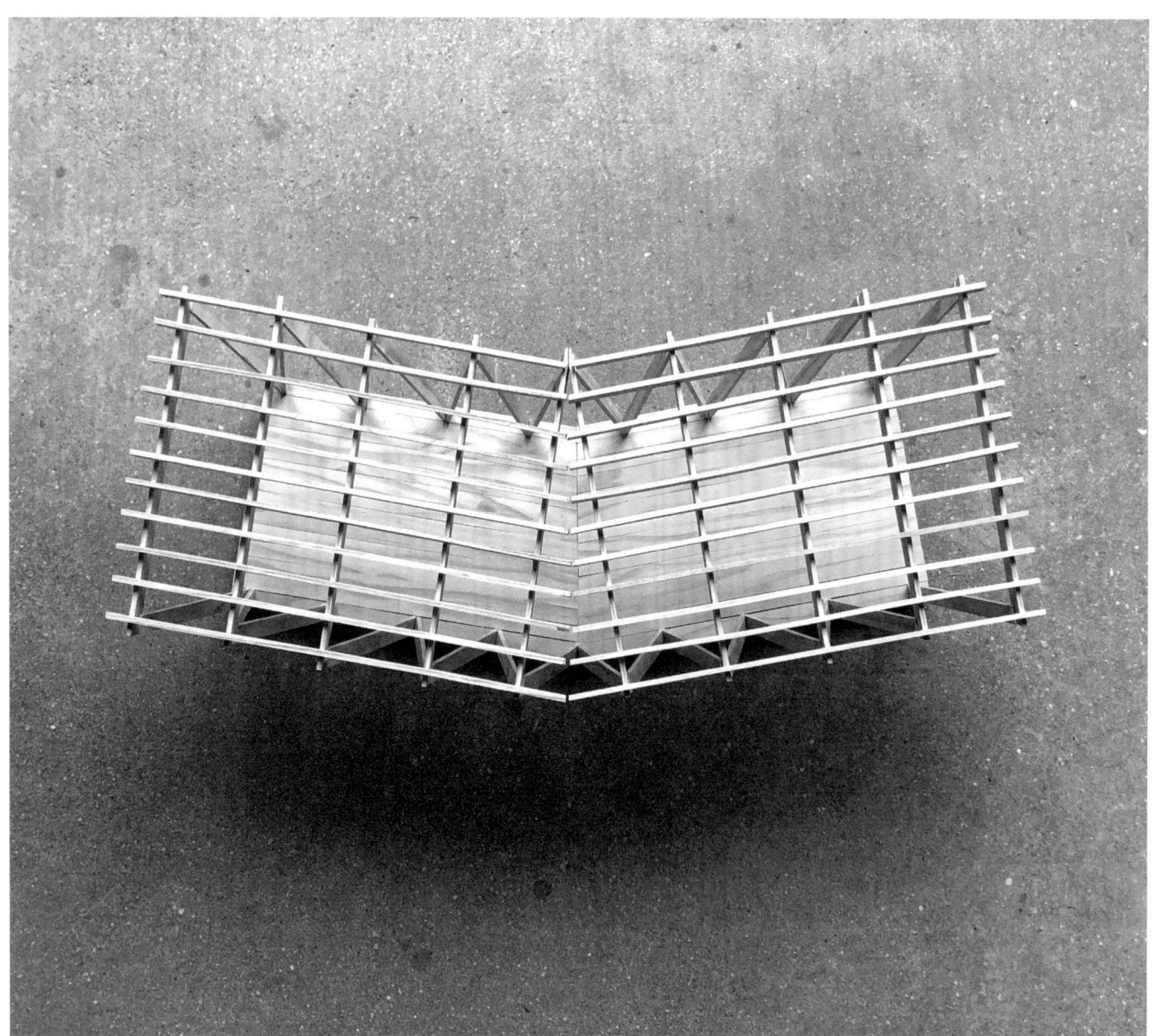

Model seen from above.

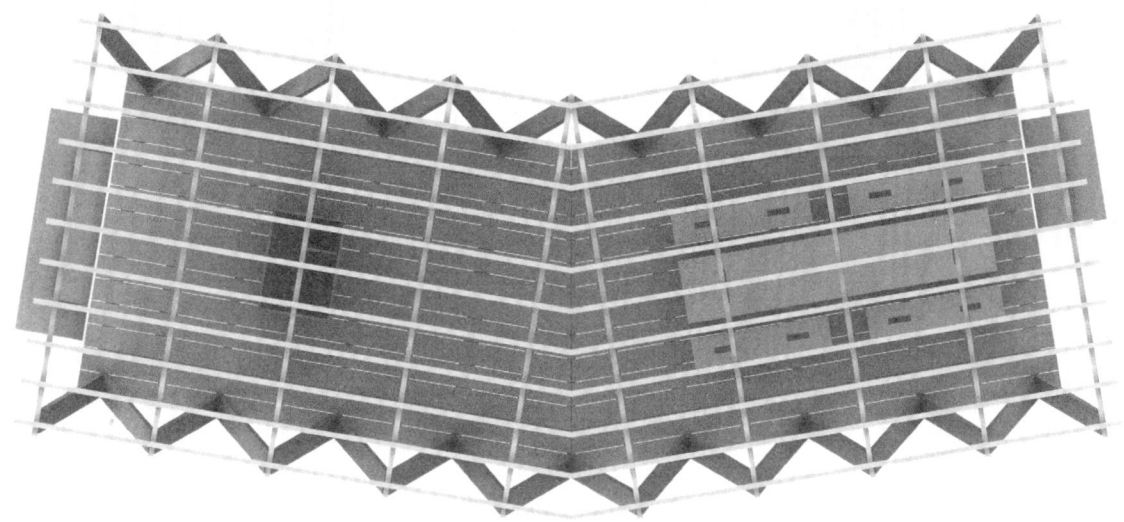

Plan 1:100.

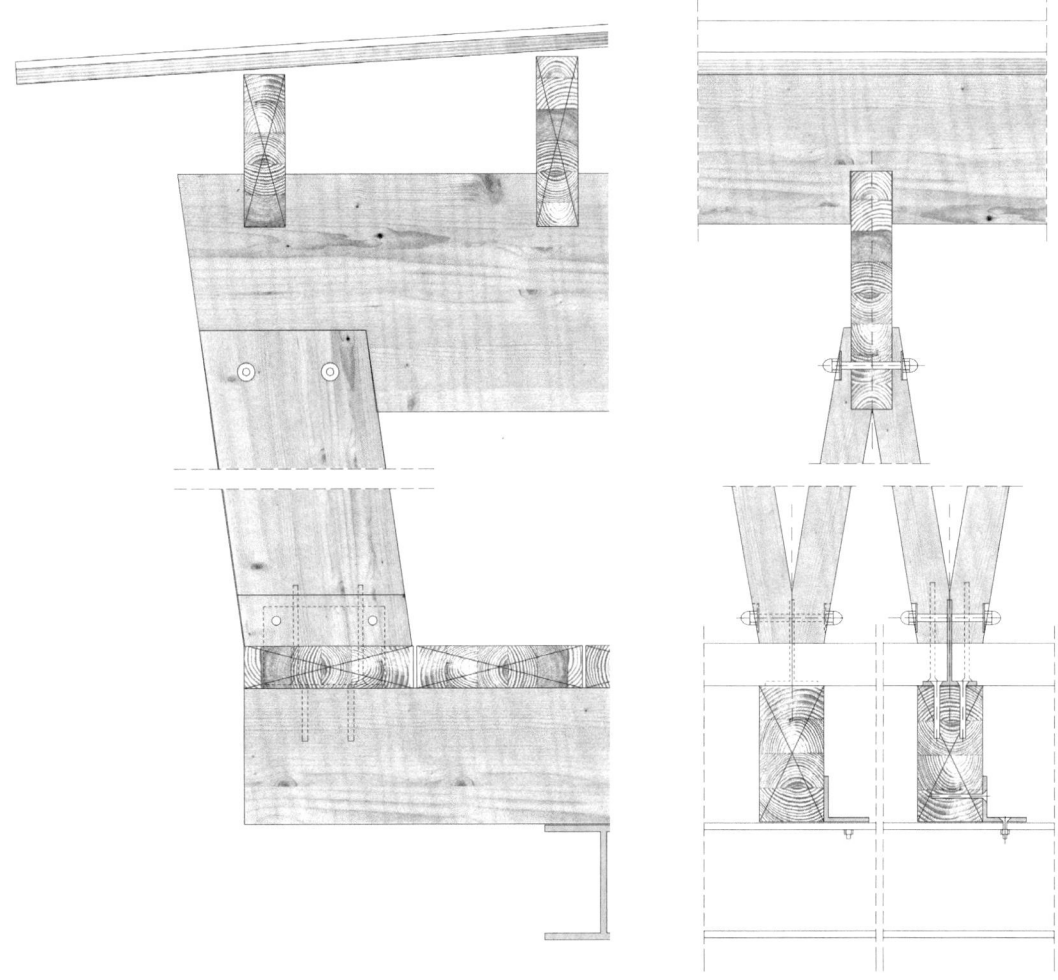

(opposite page)
View of Loggia d'Ombra
in Serra dei Giardini.

Details 1:10.

Loggia Furniture

For Loggia d'Ombra we also developed a set of furniture. The geometry of the pavilion is the basis for the design of the furniture: a bench, a table and a cabinet. The legs are formed in such a way that when paired and connected with a massive piece of wood, creating the bench and table surfaces, they are locked and balanced by each other. The furniture is also a play with materiality in a long tradition of materials acting as something else. In the history of architecture there are many instances to be found of stone mimicking wood, wood mimicking stone, and cast iron mimicking stone as well as wood. The Serra dei Giardini greenhouse is from the period when cast iron was used to resemble wooden structures. For the Loggia Furniture we made wooden parts for the legs, which were sandblasted so that when cast in iron a clear imprint of the wood appears on their surface. (2018)

Wooden plug and cast iron leg for bench.

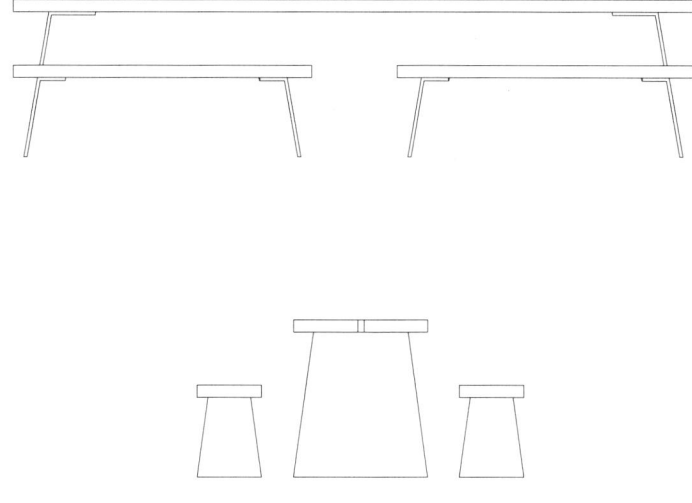

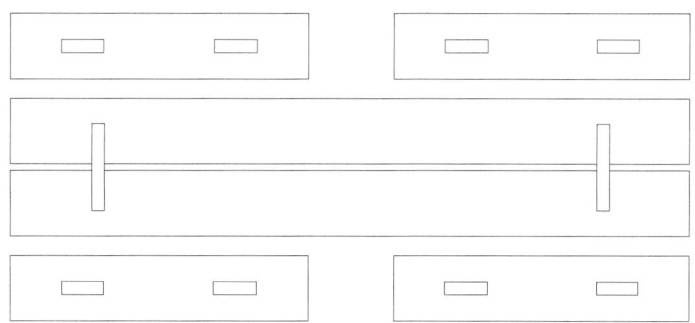

Drawings 1:20.

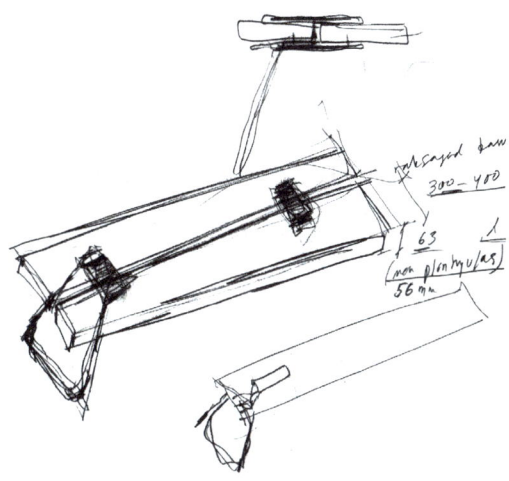

(opposite page)
Bench and table
in Loggia d'Ombra.

(left)
Sketch of structural
principle for the bench.

(right)
Mock-up of loggia
bench 1:1.

Ör Pavilion

Parallel to Loggia d'Ombra for the Venice Architecture Biennale, a sister pavilion was developed. This pavilion was to function as a place for public dialogue during an urban planning process in the Stockholm area. To extend the use of the pavilion and adapt it to the Swedish climate, a translucent polycarbonate skin was added to make it possible to heat it temporarily. What started as the simple idea of copying the structure turned out to be a slightly more complex process since snow loads and possible wind loads generated by the closed walls had to be considered. In the end the new parameters affected only the metal fixings—the dimensions of the glulam components stayed the same. The Loggia Furniture that was on display in Venice as prototypes was now in production and could be installed in the pavilion. (2019)

Exterior view—adding light to the neighborhood.

(opposite page)
Interior view of Ör Pavilion with Loggia Furniture.

Rosendal Pavilion

When the Ör Pavilion had served its purpose, the process of finding it a new home started. The aim was to find a place for it in an area of Stockholm where it could be publicly accessible. Rosendals Garden on the island of Djurgården was our first choice, and it turned out that the structure, originally designed in relation to a garden with a greenhouse in Venice, had a character that also suited its Swedish equivalent. Historically the hunting grounds of the Swedish royal family, Djurgården has long since been transformed into a green outdoor living room for Stockholmers, with generous parks and cultural institutions. The gardens of the little Rosendal Palace were designed in the same English garden tradition as the Giardini in Venice, and on many sites on Djurgården smaller buildings and pavilions act as focal points in the landscape. The long Swedish tradition of building in wood is also very present in these buildings, each of them built according to the architectonic ideals and available building techniques of their times. Supplying a contemporary addition to this tradition was a very attractive notion to all involved parties. After a long dialogue with the City Planning Office, supported by the landscape architects working on the renovation plan for the garden, an attractive placement adjacent to the orchard was agreed upon and a building permit was granted. On its new site, the pavilion will be open to visitors as well as act as an important space for Rosendals Garden to use in its daily educational work, spreading knowledge on how we can shift to a sustainable society. (2022)

121

The pavilion painted in Djurgården green and fitted with stairs and a ramp formed to make space for dead wood, providing homes for insects and small animals to support local biodiversity.

At the Rosendals Garden, the pavilion was placed at the end of the orchard, activating a lesser-used part of the garden. Close enough to the kitchen to be practical and far enough from the café and shop to have some privacy.

Klockelund

The project for the Lakeside Houses of Klockelund ran in parallel to our work on the Loggia d'Ombra. The balconies are a key element of the project, and we consulted with structural engineers to create detailing that ensures their appearance over time. Our experiences on the pavilion projects fed into this process. The balcony structure is formed from diagonal glulam beams and CLT slabs. Increasing the dimension of the wood secures the static function and ensures fire safety, and cladding can be avoided. Details are formed to make sure that water is not retained and that the structure dries fast after rain. The CLT slabs are exposed in the ceilings of the balconies and painted in a semi-transparent white to reflect light into the apartments. The structure of the house is of prefabricated wooden volumetric elements, and a green roof will detain rainwater and help biodiversity. The fire-protected wood facade will turn gray over time. The project is part of a development along Drevviken lake and the greater densification plan for the suburb of Farsta in southern Stockholm. Although Farsta was planned and built in the 1950s and 1960s according to the Swedish modernist concept of the ABC city, its architecture is very rich and detailed for its time, due to the work of renowned architects Backström & Reinius. Their buildings, which we have studied before, also provided inspiration for our work here.

The five urban villas with sixty-five apartments are placed in a row along the shoreline. The site previously housed light industry and commercial facilities, which have had to make way for new housing in what will become an attractive area close to nature, local centers and the subway. An adjoining area of allotment gardens with smaller houses inspired us to also provide generous outdoor spaces for the future inhabitants, making large balconies the key element of the project. The public area of each apartment, the combined kitchen and living room, is placed along the balcony facade, expanding the indoor area to the outdoors, which also provides the possibility of having a small "garden" although you are not living at ground level. (2015–ongoing)

(opposite page)
View of the facades with balconies facing the lake. Balconies formed from glulam pillars and CLT slabs.

Site plan of the new development as a whole 1:2500.

Klockelund facades
1:400.

View from the wetland bordering the lake in front of the houses.

Pavilions on Tour

128

When the Biennale was over and the Loggia d'Ombra had been taken down, our client planned to bring the pavilion to the grounds of the UN Headquarters in Nairobi as a display of wooden architecture and as a place for seminars during the first UN Habitat Assembly. Although it was carefully packed in a container, transportation was a challenge and it did not reach Nairobi in time. The pavilion was instead offered to the Swedish Embassy, and now has a place at the Swedish Embassy residence in Nairobi, where it will once again be a place for meetings and education, as well as celebrations and weddings.

Since the Venice pavilion did not arrive on time, a pavilion made of locally sourced wood had to be erected on the grounds of UN— its working name was "Panic Pavilion" as it had to be planned and built in a week. We chose to build it out of boards with a single dimension and without any metal fittings except screws. A simple, repetitive structure to host talks and an exhibition on Agenda 2030, the "Panic Pavilion" also got a new life after the UN Habitat Assembly.

An unbuilt corner next to a water station was cleared in Mathare and the pavilion was furnished with benches in order to become a public gathering point. To protect it from termites and water damage, the lower part meeting the ground was treated with bitumen. (2019)

The experience from Nairobi inspired a version for Skellefteå in Sweden to house an exhibition on Agenda 2030 and the challenges faced by the building industry to meet these demands. Again, it was built out of wooden profiles with only one singular dimension. (2019)

(opposite page)
Pavilion in
Mathare, Nairobi.

Pavilion in
Skellefteå.

Le Pavillion Hexagonal

Le Pavillon Hexagonal is a pavilion to meet, talk, dine and discuss in. For us it was a development of Loggia d'Ombra and was designed specifically for the garden of the Swedish Institute in the Marais in Paris. The geometry is inspired by the fact that the hexagon is a metaphor for France, and we developed this idea further in search of a structural logic. The pavilion is an investigation of the triangle as a geometric shape as well as a static principle and how it can be joined together to create space. A self-supporting geometry is created by joining the wooden triangular frames along their sides. The exposed foundation lifts the wooden floor to seating height, providing visitors with an informal place to sit under the roof all around the pavilion. The details and fittings are designed to facilitate assembly and disassembly, allowing the pavilion to be easily erected in new places. The structure is built in Swedish pine, planed to slender profiles and tinted with a silver glaze to heighten the character of the material and to interact with the changing light throughout the day. (2021)

(left)
Le Pavillon Hexagonal being assembled in Paris.

(right)
Inauguration party in the garden of the Swedish Institute in Paris.

(opposite page)
In the garden of the 16th-century palace housing the Swedish Institute.

Le Pavillon Hexagonal,
Paris, 2022.

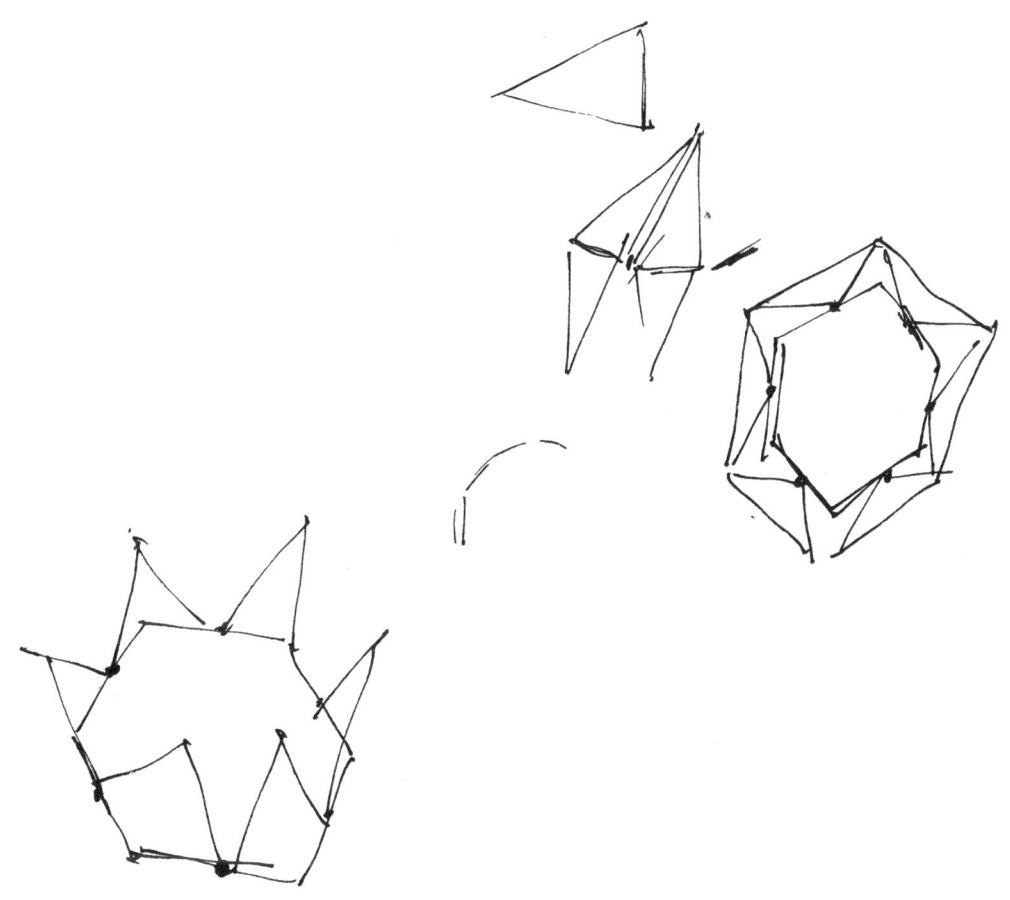

Early sketches of
Le Pavillon Hexagonal.

Hexagon H22

An oak block joining the glulam diagonals.

Having created a long series of exhibition pavilions, we were happy to continue the process in consultation with a produce to develop a pavilion for their catalogue. The producer sensed a growing interest in semi-protected outdoor structures as places for both work and social interaction and was keen to develop Le Pavillon Hexagonal into a product. Hexagon H22 was displayed for the first time at theexhibition H22 in Helsingborg, and we envisage possible placements in private gardens as well as common spaces in housing developments and public parks. The structure is formed of glulam triangles mounted onto each other, forming a stable geometric structure with wooden oak distances. The roof is made of Swedish heartwood pine shingles. (2022)

Hexagon H22
on display at H22
in Helsingborg.

Lamp Cercle, designed for the pavilion by Marie-Louise Hellgren.

Hexagon H22 roof clad with high-quality pine shingles.

Bridge Kattvikskajen

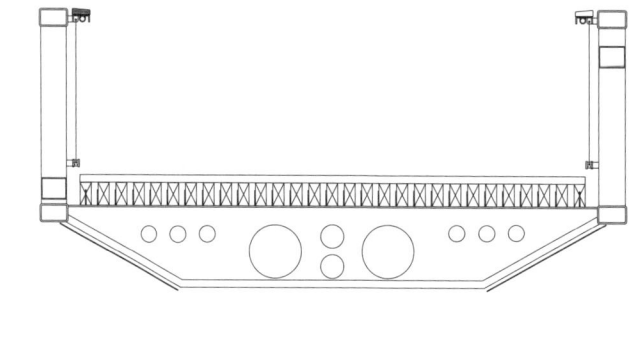

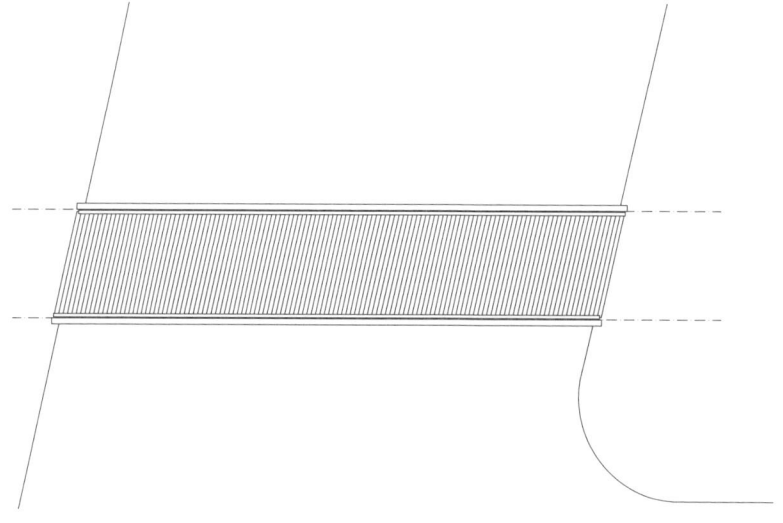

Over a small canal in the city of Hudiksvall connecting a row of small red harbor sheds to the ocean, a new pedestrian and bike bridge was needed. The sides of the bridge that carry the floor are formed as Warren trusses in steel with a slight arch to provide a characteristic light silhouette. The girders are painted red to match the adjacent Falu red sheds. The floor is made of massive wooden planks and the handrail in oak provides a soft, welcoming touch to pedestrians. In order to be as transparent as possible and to let the character of the girders stand out, the fall protection is provided by a stainless-steel net. Lamps providing downlight onto the floor were integrated under the handrail. To visually minimize the substructure of the bridge, which incorporates space for district heating pipes for the adjacent new housing, the sides of the substructure slope and are clad with stainless-steel plates that reflect the water surface below. (2022)

(opposite page)
Bridge Kattvikskajen,
section 1:50, plan 1:250.

View of the bridge from the entrance of the canal. Girders in Falu red, with stainless-steel plates underneath the walkway reflecting the light of the water.

Double House

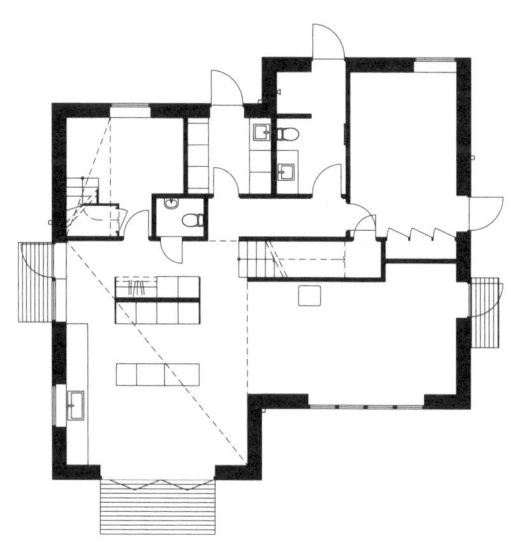

140

A home for a small family outside Trosa. Our client wanted a building that would blend in with the nature of the site, characterized by exposed rocks softened by inland ice and areas of untouched landscape with small trees. The regulation plan allowed for a footprint of 120 square meters and a pitched roof, making a second story possible. To break down the scale of the house we designed it as two volumes with slightly shifted plans. The kitchen and living room are placed to the south toward the view of the sea. The cross-section of the house is exposed in full height, providing circulation and dividing the open social areas from the private bedrooms to the north, where the greenery of the site creates privacy. The colours of the site provided the colour scheme of the building. The wooden facade is patinated and slightly pigmented to a light gray, in dialogue with the rocks, and the windows are orange, echoing the characteristic and beautiful lichen that grows on the rocks. (2023)

Plan and Section 1:200.

(opposite page)
The kitchen, a double-height space. Ash floor and white wooden panels on walls and roof.

View from the sea. Exterior with colors inspired by the site—a light gray wooden facade and orange windows.

Interacting Spaces

Stockholm City Library

The Stockholm Public Library from 1928 by architect Gunnar Asplund was to be revitalized. The scope of the project was an ambitious renovation of the building and the historic interior spaces, the integration of the bazaars toward Sveavägen, as well as a new children's area below the rotunda. The project was a collaboration, with architects Caruso St John and Gatun responsible for the building work and us together with Nyréns Arkitektkontor and Unik Fabrik as the architects of the library organization. The integration of the bazaars into the library entailed adding a new, generous space facing Sveavägen to become a new "living room" for the library, with entrance functions and a multiuse space for events, lectures and performances, as well as reading spaces and a café. This was an attractive and ambitious plan to create a contemporary extension of the City Library onto the street and make it more accessible and open, connecting to the street life outside. Our task was to design the interiors of all the new public areas, as well as to guarantee the functionality of the library in all parts of the project. Besides the bazaar area, a large focus was the new children's area under the existing rotunda. In the design of the spaces as well as the furniture we sought dialogue with the strict geometry of Asplund's design as well as the richness of detail. Like in Asplund's time we also turned to natural materials and Swedish handicraft traditions. In order to get a child's perspective on what the future library should be, we held a number of workshops with children of different ages in the course of the design process. (2016–2018)

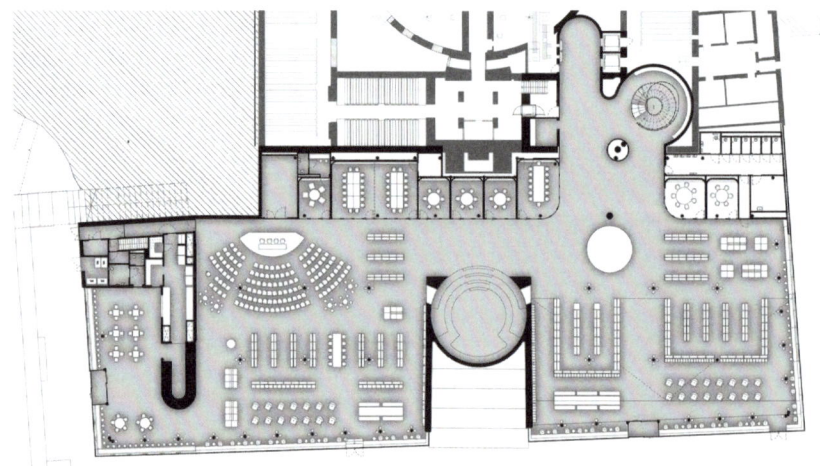

(previous spread)
Exterior view—the bazaars creating a new public area, opening up the library toward Sveavägen.

(opposite page above)
Elevation toward Odengatan.

(opposite page below)
Plan of the bazaars 1:800.

Interior view of the reading area in the bazaars.

Workshop model of the new children's rotunda (below the main rotunda).

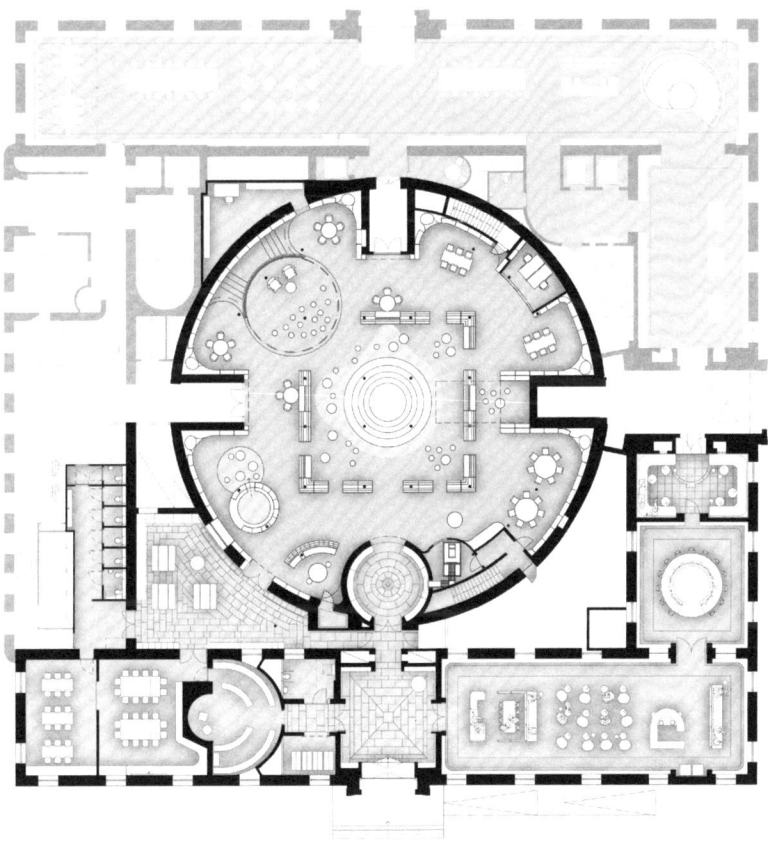

Floor plan of the children's rotunda adjacent to the existing children's area 1:500.

DIS Stockholm

A new school in Stockholm was needed for the Danish Institute for Study Abroad (DIS). DIS provides international, mostly North American, bachelor's students with an international student experience as part of their education. The school is located in the new building of the Royal Academy of Music. Since our client signed the contract for the space before its completion, we had the opportunity to develop a layout suited to the needs of the school. The project had high demands from an environmental perspective, with an environmental classification system setting the parameters for our work. The school is situated on four floors in the back wings of the building. One area is for staff, with offices and a faculty lounge, and three are for students, including classrooms and student lounges. We arranged the area around a spatial core, a thick wall clad in Douglas fir veneer that incorporated wiring as well as ventilation and storage, with some sections formed as seating niches and for printers and computers. For diversity and orientation, linoleum floors were chosen with a different color scheme for each of the four different spaces. (2016)

Seating niche and storage in the central wall, clad in Douglas fir veneer.

(opposite page)
View of the student lounge outside the classrooms.

WY13

Infill projects are quite rare in Stockholm. On the site of this project on Södermalm, an old one-story industrial brick building had been demolished. A requirement for the new building was to integrate a memory of the previous structure. Rather than trying to rebuild the historic facade, a task we deemed would not lead to a satisfying result, we proposed a replica of the entrance portico to be cast in concrete on site. The program was that of a boutique hotel with small but characteristic rooms and a large, high space to serve breakfast, function as a restaurant and host small concerts that could be open onto the street. The glass facade toward the street contrasts starkly with the neighboring older buildings, and through reflections in the glass a valuable complexity is created. We used a glazing system with hidden profiles, railings in brass, and gutters and pipes in copper for a warm character. (2014)

Street facade, where the portico cast on site in concrete is a memory of the earlier building on the site.

Gypsum model
of portico.

(opposite page)
Close-up of the concrete portico replica
and the curtain wall glass facade with
balcony railings in brass.

Gotlandshem

This was a design for an invited competition that we won, but was never realized. The task was to design a new headquarters for Gotlandshem, a public housing company based on Gotland, an island in the Baltic Sea. The program was complex, involving offices, workshops, a garage, flats for temporary use by tenants during renovation, as well as commercial spaces. Our proposal was inspired by an interpretation of the traditional Gotlandsgård farmstead, with an enclosed inner courtyard creating a generous wind-protected outdoor area. As the jury formulated it: "The proposal presents a comprehensive design and composition that convincingly provides an inviting meeting and workplace. The buildings, on an intimate scale, are an innovative interpretation of the small-town typology that contributes nicely to the emerging area. Volumes that interact with their surroundings, with an expression of kindness, warmth and openness. The semi-open block is oriented around the inviting garden and courtyard, which provides a nice spatial order and has the potential to become a meeting place. The surfaces can be used during different seasons and weather thanks to weather-protected seating which provides conditions for increased outdoor living." The social and ecological sustainability aims were ambitious, and we designed a building with a structure in wood, glulam and CLT, a wooden facade, and solar panels integrated into the roof. We planned for a high degree of prefabrication, as well as a system that would be flexible over time. The project was a collaboration with Waugh Thistleton Architects and Land Arkitektur. (2020)

(opposite page)
Section 1:500. Cut through the green courtyard, the hub of the project.

View of the entrance opening up to the buildings and the courtyard.

The inner courtyard is wind-protected, creating an attractive microclimate.

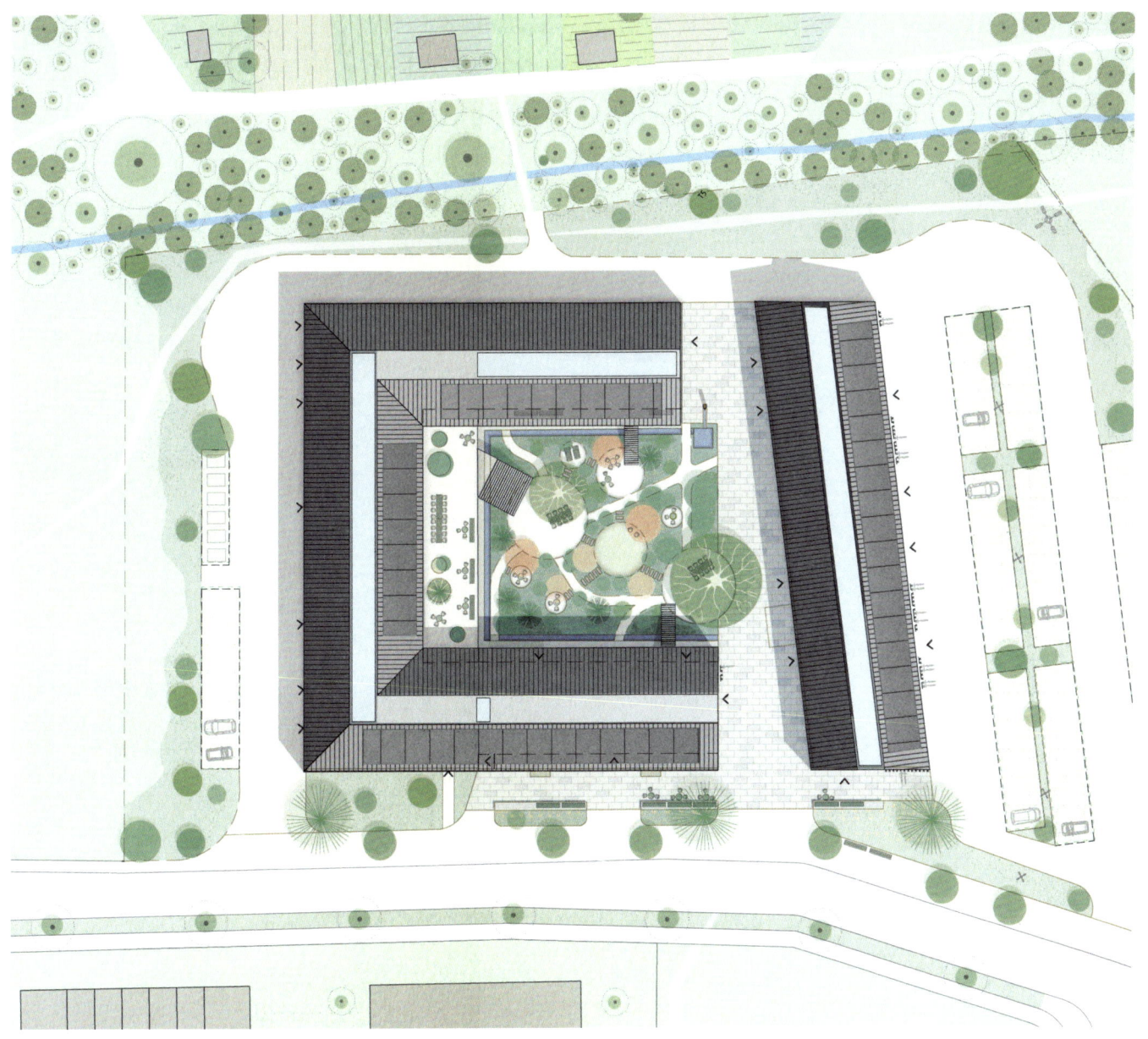

Site plan 1:800. The central courtyard with both green and paved areas can be reached from all parts of the building.

View of the open office area on the second floor, opening up to the terrace that links the space to the courtyard. A flexible space with characteristic Y-pillars and light from the roof lantern.

Section 1:250. Cars below
and an open office space with
terrace above.

The Cords & Co

The Cords & Co, a start-up fashion brand devoted to corduroy, approached us to develop a concept and design for their retail environment. Their stores, all set to open at the same time as the launch of the brand, were to be located in Stockholm, Paris, London, Los Angeles and New York. From the beginning, we felt a strong attraction to The Cords' vision of working with corduroy as a material with a distinct identity. Creating a physical presence around that particular fabric, drawing from its heritage and character, was an interesting starting point for our architectural exploration. Inspired by the client's strategy of reviving a traditional material and bringing it to broader use, we approached the architectonic elements in the same manner, forming traditional materials into new expressions. With a strategy inspired by Adolf Loos's technique of having the material itself create the ornament, the design is built on a palette of materials with natural expressive properties: MDF, brass, mirrors, linen and neon. Like corduroy, the materials are worked and connected so as to create a composition of lines, overlaid in different scales. Through careful detailing, cheaper materials like the MDF become elevated, and more exclusive materials, such as brass, are toned down. The MDF unfolds like a ribbon of fabric that brings verticality to the small spaces and softens the corners. The mirrors are cut in wide strips, flat or angled, to reflect the space in vertical segments. Inspired by artists working with neon lights as their medium, we were able to harness artificial light to turn it into a tectonic feature. Through the use of striped neon lights for the display table, we have given shape to light, reinforcing the vertical stripes present throughout in the space. (2017)

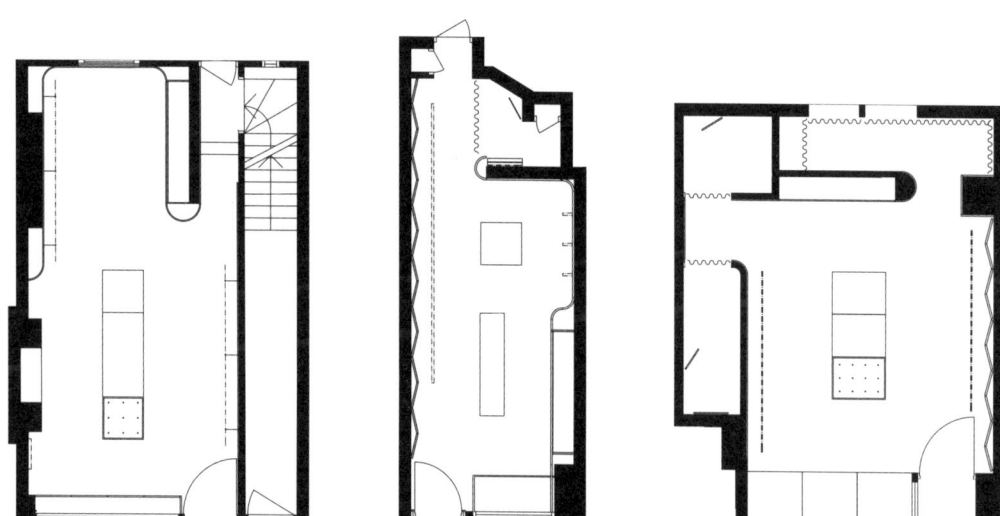

(previous spread)
MDF CNC-cut to enable
bending at The Cords Paris.

Plans 1:125 from left to right:
London, Paris, Stockholm.

(opposite page)
The Cords & Co London: changing
rooms in the basement.

The Cords' flagship store on Stureplan, Stockholm, was a small but high-ceilinged space where the verticality was emphasized by the strips of MDF. An existing pillar was clad in brass and cut-up mirrors broke up the views and expanded the space. The cashier unit was in brass and the light display table reflected the neon signage "Cords."

The Cords LA became a collaboration with graphic designer Barbara Stauffacher Solomon. Working with her was a great experience, since her whole production of Supergraphics, from her work at Sea Ranch in California to Centan in Bagarmossen, Stockholm, has fascinated us, and our collaboration deepened our understanding of her work. Barbara developed a Cords graphic for the interior that was executed by a skilled sign painter directly onto the wall.

The Parisian space was typical of the Marais: a very condensed room open to a narrow street, with a traditional facade painted white. A softly curved MDF wall flowed along the right-hand wall. The cuts in the MDF created vertical lines, an echo of the structure of corduroy. Opposite, the angled mirror wall ran the entire depth of the space. Rather than mirroring the space, the tilted reflections broke up the views. The neon installation evokes a skate ramp, a subculture intimately bound to the history of corduroy.

In London the deep space was given a diversification in character to create a spatial sequence from the street to the garden in the back. The classic London store front was kept and brought inside for the window display, which was also painted black. The first part of the space was dominated by an old mantelpiece, which was painted black and fitted with shelves. Opposite it was a mirror wall that widened the space and reflected the mantelpiece. The brass cashier and display table with a neon mirror installation, mirroring neon "cords," was the focus of the space. The back part of the store was fitted with MDF, enclosing the space and framing the view to the garden in the back. In the basement housing the dressing room and events space, subdivisions were created with textile draperies.

(opposite page)
The Cords & Co Stockholm
store at Stureplan.

(left)
The Cords & Co Paris store
in the Marais.

(right)
The Los Angeles store, a collaboration
with Barbara Stauffacher Solomon,
the inventor of Supergraphics as
seen at Sea Ranch, California.

Let Me Be Myself

An exhibition on the life of Anne Frank and what we can learn from it, produced by the Anne Frank House, was given a specific design for its display at the Living History Forum in Stockholm and for a further tour in Sweden. The structure of the exhibition entailed a chronological history overlapping personal reflections from Frank's diary and her family's history with the development of the war. Our strategy for the design was to work with the overlapping of the personal and the historic in a visual manner, too, with prints on transparent textiles and polycarbonate fitted in thin wooden frames. Pictures of the two stories are overlaid and merged into one. The frames were built in a set of shifting radiuses, creating a system making it possible to shape enclosing spaces in different locations. (2015)

Let Me Be Myself—The Life Story of Anne Frank. Traveling exhibition on its first stop at the Living History Forum in Stockholm.

Close-up of the wooden frames in which polycarbonate boards could be inserted or textile prints mounted.

Stockholm Winebar

Our client Stockholm Ost & Chark was opening a cheese and delicatessen store with a wine bar on Södermalm. The store is on the ground floor of an apartment building from 1958 by architects Klemming & Thelaus, on the busy intersection of Bondegatan and Renstiernas gata. For the concept and choice of materials we were inspired by the products in the store regarding color, materiality and structure. The structure of cheese can be smooth, grainy, airy, solid, flaky or crumbly. The comparison with wood is also often made when describing the characteristics of wine as having acidity, sweetness, fruitiness, phenols and tannins. Another important point of departure was the structure of the site itself. The beautiful teak frames and oak benches of the existing windows were restored and the classic black-and-white checkered tiled floor was kept. Together the green color of the ceiling and walls creates a backdrop for the furniture, products and details. For added elements we chose to work with materials that are strong in character and age beautifully, such as birch plywood, oak, brass and leather. (2018)

Close-up of window seating.

(opposite page)
Close-up of entrance area.

Oak and leather seating along the oak-framed windows — product display in green-stained plywood.

(left)
The *chambre séparée*. The checkered floor was installed by the former tenant and integrated into the new design.

(right)
Bar in stained plywood, solid oak and brass.

Bio Rio

Our local cinema—one of the last independent cinemas left in Stockholm—got a new owner with new ideas. The adjacent bar and restaurant had already been opened up toward the cinema lobby but it lacked atmosphere. Built in the 1930s, the lobby was clad in teak veneer, a material we had worked with previously, and, again, we sought inspiration there. Large investments had already been made in the bar and kitchen, so many parts had to stay the same and resources were limited. Our strategy included a few strong additions and the wrapping of the space in a warm color. In order to make the bar the centerpiece of the space we developed a new design for the customer side of the bar in solid oak, reusing darker butterfly joints from earlier projects. We were able to increase its length a little, and the glass rack extending across the length of the bar strengthens its presence. For a warmer character, the color white was eliminated on all surfaces except the tabletops, making them the focus of the space (a strategy learnt from the Four Seasons restaurant in New York designed by Philip Johnson). (2021)

View from the cinema foyer into the bar and restaurant.

(opposite page)
The bar front in solid oak with butterfly joints of smoked oak.

Close-up of cinema desk seen with the original wooden panel in the stairs down to the cinema. The stainless steel mirrors the butterfly joint, making it whole.

Seating integrated
into the window niche.

Visitor Center

One out of four similar spaces, the café was cleared of additional fixtures and fitted with new benches and tables in solid pine. Stools designed by Gunnar Asplund.

The Woodland Cemetery (1916–40) in Stockholm by Gunnar Asplund and Sigurd Lewerentz is an architectural landmark that became a Unesco World Heritage site in 1994. Our task was to renovate the cemetery's utility building by Asplund to its original state, conveying the quality of the interior spaces. Built as a grain store for the cemetery as well as being used by women from Dalarna who came for seasonal work, it now functions as a café and information center for visitors. It is a remarkable building with "out of the ordinary" proportions in the exterior volume as well as the inner spaces. Taking a gentle approach, we stripped the space of disrespectful additions and created new wooden furniture for the reception area that is simple in character but fine in detail. By lucky coincidence, a stool designed by Asplund had just gone into production again and so could be used to furnish the seminar space, along with some tables and benches of our own design. (2009)

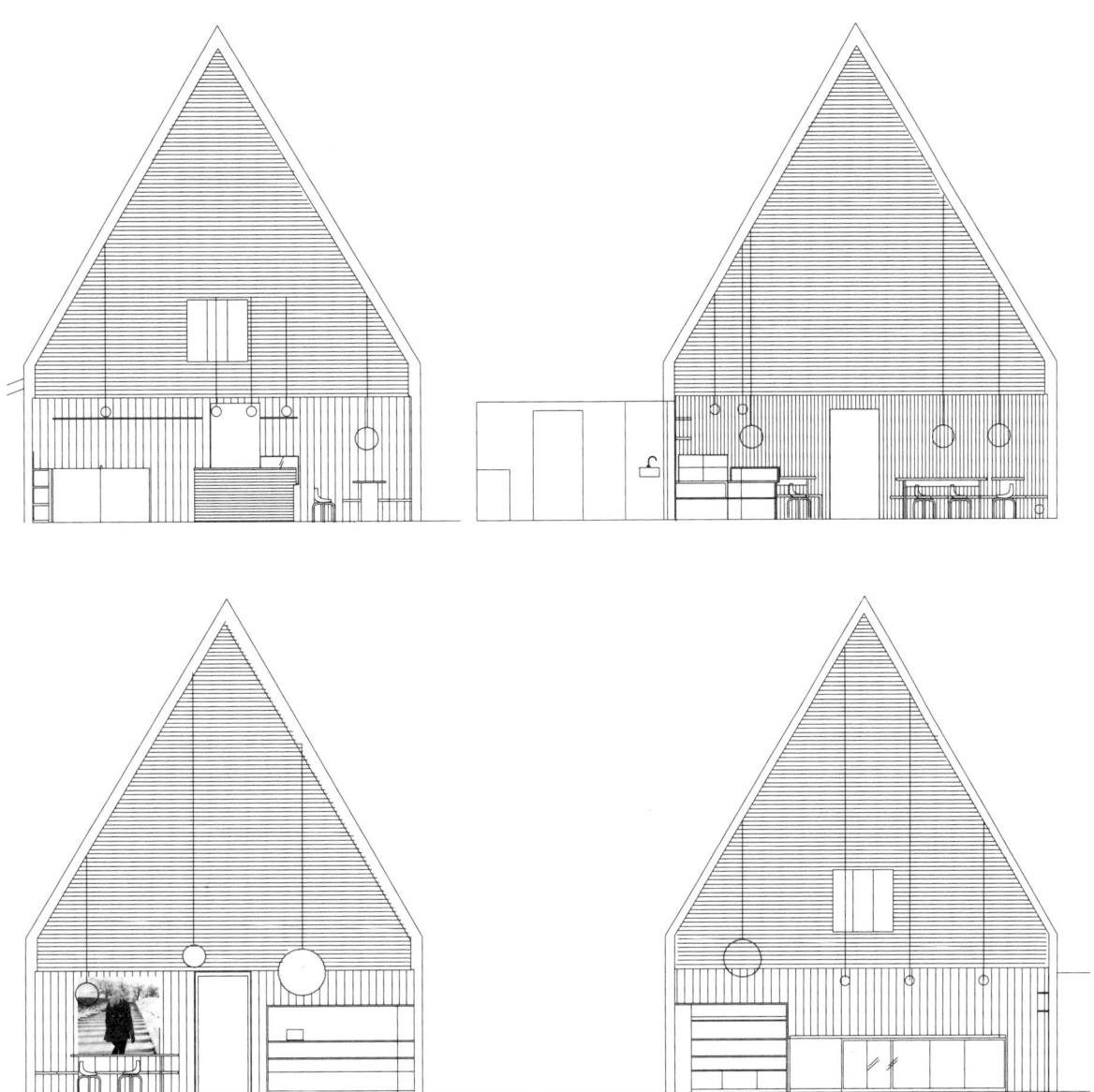

Sections 1:125. The café was given a new interior display, a desk and a bookstore corner adjusted to the existing window and stairs.

Ulriksdal Cemetery

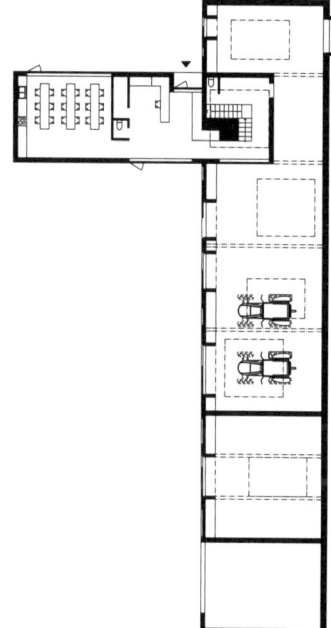
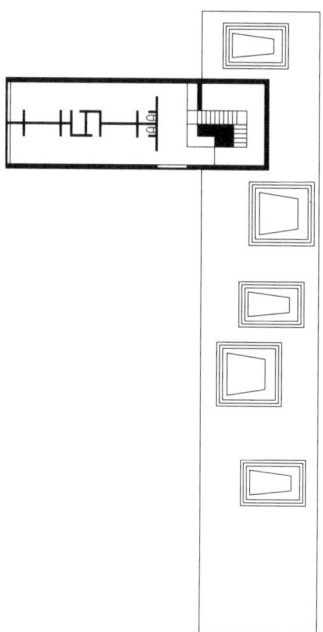

The cemetery maintenance building at Ulriksdal, Solna, is formed of two volumes set at an angle, open to the northwest and supplemented with an ancillary building. The volume of the workshop reaches up toward a slope where oak trees grow. The long concrete facade with its relief effect stretches out to form a backdrop for the cemetery and separates its tranquility from the activity of the working courtyard of the service building. The building also forms an entryway into the park and cemetery. It is a building that states its practical function and draws on industrial aesthetics but that also expresses something of the pride and ease that resonates in the free design of the cemetery. The service building consists of two different volumes in two different materials, concrete and wood, holding each other. Where the two volumes meet, the staircase constitutes a hub linking the workshops, administration and staff areas. The stairwell has a skylight, bringing light into the very core of the structure. The service building is constructed out of materials that will age naturally and beautifully. The concrete stairs and the floors are cast in place, and by choice the traces and defects from the casting process have been left visible. The prefabricated concrete elements of the facade show both their faces: the smooth faces outwards and the coarser faces inwards. Wooden facades and interior walls are built out of long boards of fir. The structure has passive, natural ventilation and geothermal heating. The green roof is made of sedum while the detailing is zinc. The inner courtyard facade, with its recessed doors and the windows of the administration unit, provides a quiet workspace as well as the opportunity to see into the administration building. (A collaboration with Petra Gipp.) (2009)

182

(previous spread left)
Plan first and second floor 1:500.

(previous spread right)
The central staircase, cast in concrete on site, leads to the upper staff rooms.

The facade facing the memorial site with shadows of trees against the closed white prefab concrete wall.

The facades toward the working courtyard are clad in wooden panels now turned gray. Generous windows open up to the entrance and reception area while the workshop space receives light from the roof lanterns.

The staff area on the upper floor
has been afforded large windows.

Roof lanterns provide good lighting in the workshop area. Interior windows connect the workshop to the entrance and the rooms above.

Tower of Democracy

A prototype for a new type of public building was developed as part of an exhibition in Sege Park, Malmö, on the theme of supporting the commons. The theme we chose was local democracy and, more specifically, power and a sense of ownership over one's surroundings. Throughout history, power has been manifested by verticality; the view from above has often been reserved for economic or political power. In tall buildings that dominate the skyline of the city, people have been able to look out over the landscape at their feet. In Malmö, a city where power is shared with everyone, the highest point is also open to many. The tower of Sege Park is a sign of what we want to accomplish with each other. A wooden core is enveloped by a staircase that leads to the viewpoint. Inside the core is a theater, a round, non-hierarchical, warm room that is open and empty for flexible use in order to support local democracy.
(2017)

(opposite page)
Section. A contribution to the exhibition *Commoning Kits* for Sege Park in Malmö.

Model.

Index

Project	Client	Location, date	Pg.
Aesop Bibliotekstan	Aesop	Stockholm, 2014	42
Aesop SoFo	Aesop	Stockholm, 2016	46
Artbarn	Sjödell	Roslagen, 2014	54
Atelier Grytnäs	Katarina Lundeberg	Lisö, 2020	28
Bio Rio	Indio Studio	Stockholm, 2021	174
Bridge Kattvikskajen	City of Hudiksvall	Hudiksvall, 2022	138
Ca d'Ombra	SI, KS Ark, Folkhem	Venice, 2016	103
DIS Stockholm	DIS	Stockholm, 2016	150
Double House	Private	Trosa, 2023	140
Elma	Finnish Museum of Architecture	Venice, 2012	40
Gotlandshem	Gotlandshem	Visby, 2020	156
Guldboda	Private	Haninge, 2009	78
Hexagon H22	Swedish Wood, Architects Sweden, Nola	Helsingborg, 2022	134
In Praise of Loos Loft	Private	Stockholm, 2013	74
Kayak House	Katarina Lundeberg	Lisö, 2018	22
KIKA Landsort	Landsort Maritime and Environmental Center	Landsort, 2014	88
Klockelund	Folkhem	Stockholm, 2014–	124
Let Me Be Myself	The Living History Forum	Stockholm, Uppsala, Rydal, 2015	168
Le Pavillon Hexagonal	SI, Swedish Wood, Architects Sweden	Paris, 2021	130
Lindholmen Lab	Private	Lindholmen, 2020	34
Loggia d'Ombra	SI, Swedish Wood, Architects Sweden, Folkhem	Venice, 2018; Nairobi, 2019	106
Loggia Furniture	Källemo	Venice, 2018; Ör, 2019	114
Magelungens Strand	Folkhem	Stockholm, 2016–	92
Passage of Wood	Wallpaper	Milan, Venice, Bregenzerwald, 2016	19
Pavilions on Tour	SI, Architects Sweden, Folkhem	Skellefteå, Nairobi, 2019	128
Risön Cabin	Private	Risön, 2016	70
Rosendal Pavilion	Folkhem, Veidekke	Stockholm, 2022	120
Sauna Grytnäs	Private	Lisö, 2021	50
Solbrinken	Private	Nacka, 2009	61
Stockholm City Library	City of Stockholm	Stockholm, 2018–2020	145
Stockholm Winebar	Stockholm Ost & Chark	Stockholm, 2018	170
Storön	Private	Stockholm, 2016	82
The Cords & Co	The Cords & Co	Worldwide, 2017	162
Tower of Democracy	KS Ark	Malmö, Sege Park 2017	186
Tree House	Folkhem	Sundbyberg, 2020–	56
Ulriksdal Cemetery	Solna Kyrkogårdsförvaltning	Solna, 2010	180
Vega	Stena Bygg	Haninge, 2022	96
Visitor Center	Stockholms Kyrkogårdsförvaltning	Stockholm, 2009	178
WY13	Hotel Hellsten	Stockholm, 2014	152
Ör Pavilion	Folkhem, Veidekke	Sundbyberg, 2019	118

Builder	Engineer/Construction	Collaborators
Öhmans Bygg	—	Lies-Marie Hoffmann, PS Lab, Simon Klenell
Öhmans Bygg, Solosumisura	—	PS Lab, Simon Klenell
LH Bygg	Will Jones KLH, Limträteknik	KLH, Hajom
Kamil Kasprzak, Knut Kringstad	Magnus Emilsson—Limträteknik	Södra, Dinesen, Weber, Let there be light
Daniel Garnbeck	—	Perfecta
Sjölins Smide	Hans Franklin—WSP	Landskapslaget
—	—	—
NCC, Frapont	—	Akademiska Hus, AIX
Moderna Trähus	Martin Strandell, Ramböll	—
Lies-Marie Hoffmann	—	Royal Djurgården, Peter Mackeith, Julia Kauste
—	Markus Lagerwall—Bjerking, Ramböll	Waugh Thistleton, LAND Arkitektur
Svanberg Bygg AB	Peter Bojrup-Structor	Petra Gipp Arkitektur
Sture	Ian Lund Rockliffe—Ramböll	Marie-Louise Hellgren
Blomdahls Byggservice	Hans Lanevik-Tyréns	—
Kamil Kasprzak, Knut Kringstad	Magnus Emilsson—Limträteknik	Dinesen
—	Henrik Zester—Tyréns	LG Nilsson
Gärahovs Bygg	Ian Lund Rockliffe, Peter Eriksson	—
Transpond	—	Anne Frank House
Mike England Timber, Sture	Ian Lund Rockliffe—Ramböll	Marie-Louise Hellgren
Kamil Kasprzak, Knut Kringstad	Magnus Emilsson—Limträteknik	Dinesen, Let there be light
Martinsons	Anders Wernborg	Ulrika Karlsson
Källemo	—	—
—	—	—
Oliver Beer—Zimmerei Beer	—	Dinesen, Werkraum Bregenzerwald
Buildher, Martinsons	—	—
—	Hans Lanevik — Tyréns	—
Martinsons, Veidekke	Catherine Carrick—Kvarteret K	Rosendals Garden, Royal Djurgården, Nivå Landskap
Östanbäck Timmerhus, Kamil Kasprzak	Östanbäck Timmerhus, Limträteknik	—
—	—	Land Arkitektur
—	Sweco	Nyréns, Unik Fabrik, Caruso St John, Gatun
Stockholm Bygg & Design	—	Dinesen
Erik Tuominen Bygg	Magnus Emilsson—Limträteknik	Dinesen, WB Trä
KS Projekt, Erison, Shawmut	—	Barbara Stauffacher Solomon, Sygns
—	—	Nora Linnros
Byggpartner i Dalarna	Ramböll, Limträteknik	LAND arkitektur, WI Landskap
Åke Sundvall	Peter Bojrup—Structor	Petra Gipp Arkitektur
NCC	Johan Gren—Kåver-Melin	Landskapslaget
Kyrkoförvaltning Skogskyrkogården	—	Pelle Ossler möbelsnickeri
Skandinaviska Glassystem	—	—
Martinsons, Veidekke	Catherine Carrick—Kvarteret K	—

In Praise of Shadows

Founding Partners & Architects

Team Architects

Fredric Benesch
Katarina Lundeberg

Björk Tryggvadottir
Lovisa Wallgren
Tobias Thiel
Gabriel Johannesson
Sanna Mattsson
Agnes Taye
Victor Perlheden
Petr Sulan
Lovisa Risberg
Roberta Gargani
Olga Engell
August Junge Halvorsen
Enrico Peduzzi
Lara Aebi
Linnea Carlebäck
Nanna Lindberg
Thomas Tuoma
Zakarias Samadi
Ivan Segato

Daniel Odentia
Vincent Bourassa
Nora Linnros
Clara Blasius
Clara Runstedt Klausen
Ginevra Chieca
Jack Dalla Santa
Sara Brask
Gustav Bergström
Agnes Rudehill Olcén
Chiara Bini
Klara Stigner
Francesco Borromeo
Alva Hult
Tobias Fennö Sandberg
Vicki Lundgaard
Katrine Jacobsen
Jarand Nå
Regula Andriuet
Veronica Crocetti
Monika Lenkmann